# World

# Army Ancestry

## Fourth Edition

## NORMAN HOLDING

### *revised and updated by* IAIN SWINNERTON

Published by
The Federation of Family History Societies (Publications) Ltd
15-16 Chesham Industrial Centre
Oram Street, Bury
Lancashire BL9 6EN

First edition 1982
Second edition 1991
Third edition 1997
Fourth edition 2003

ISBN: 1 86006 179 6

Printed and bound by the Alden Group, Osney Mead, Oxford OX2 0EF

# Contents

Two soldiers of the Machine Gun Corps. The man standing is a driver as shown by his spurs. the seated man is a regimental orderly and probably also a stretcher bearer.

# 1. INTRODUCTION

Anyone who served in the First World War 1914-18 or, as it was known at one time the "Great War", must now be over a hundred years old. Even those who were children during the war will have very little remembrance of the actual conflict. This means that already one of the most costly wars in history, in terms of soldiers' lives, is passing rapidly into the realms of family history and genealogy. For most people the question 'What did grandfather or father do in the war?' is already being asked too late. The ancestors have died leaving behind a few photos, a medal or two and hopefully a collection of reminiscences passed on to their children and grandchildren.

With over 5 million men serving in the forces from the British Isles alone and many women, both at home and overseas, in hospitals, munitions and other war work, there can be few people who did not have at least one close ancestor involved in the war.

For those who wish to record a history of their ancestors' war experiences it is almost too late. The majority of the most vital of the records, the Parish Registers of army research, have already been destroyed and no Bishop's Transcripts or copies exist. This book sets out to provide family history researchers with a list of sources available to them so that they may reconstruct the career of a soldier. Although it provides a few clues, it does not attempt to lay down any research methods as these must depend to a large extent on the individual case. Moreover, the contents are mainly concerned with army NCOs and private soldiers. Officers, being somewhat easier to deal with, are not considered except in passing. A large part is taken up with references to sources and books, although the latter is far from being a complete list. Some of the references and notes are not mentioned in the text so the reader is advised to read them all.

Throughout this book references are made to an ancestors *unit*. This means the defined body of men in which the ancestor served. It could be a regiment, battalion, company, battery, or squadron. These would, in turn, have belonged to a brigade, division, corps or army. The function and role of these are explained in Chapter 6.

# 2. THE RECORDS

During a soldier's career his name would have been written down many times. Firstly, when he joined the army and signed on. It would have appeared again on his first posting to a training unit. Later his name would have appeared on a variety of documents such as leave lists, transfers to another unit or on being posted overseas. If he had been promoted, his name would have appeared in Company Orders. If he won a medal, the recommendation would, initially, have been passed back to his Divisional Headquarters. If he was wounded, the medical orderly would have written down the details and, if killed, he would have been recorded once more even if his death took place in the mud of no-mans-land and his body was never found. Finally, if he survived, when he was discharged at the end of the war his name would have once more been recorded, including details of his service and any campaign medals he had been awarded.

With so many records compiled, in theory tracing a man over the four years of the war should be easy. Unfortunately, the numbers of men and the quantity of records involved made the task of storage too great. As a result many papers were destroyed before 1939. Those that survived the rigours of the Civil Service and the War Office suffered under Hitler's bombardment and many of these, too, are lost. The most significant of the latter was the major portion of the personnel records of the five million soldiers.

Your ancestors name can be found in the following sources.

Family records
The medal rolls.
The surviving personnel service records.
The remaining casualty lists.
The medal lists in the *London Gazette.*
The list of soldiers who died during the war.
The war graves list.
The war diaries of the unit in which he served. However, it is very rare for ordinary soldiers to be mentioned.
The death certificate in the Family Records Centre, Myddelton Street, London.

For anyone who survived the war unscathed, only the medal roll is likely to produce his name. If this lack of information does not discourage you, then the remainder of this book will provide sufficient details to build up at least a picture of the ancestor's life in the army even if at the end of the research much will be based on assumption and deduction.

## Missing Documents

The following items have been lost or destroyed or at least the author has not been able to locate them.

(a)  Pay Lists.

(b)  Orders of unit commanders to subordinate units.

Orders of unit commanders to their own units.

Part I and Part II orders.

Some orders of the larger units, i.e. corps and armies, still exist and are to be found attached to war diaries (*see* Chapter 9), either that of the originating unit or that of the recipient. Again a few HQ Papers on corps, armies and divisions can be found in WO 158. These tend to be confined to plans for big attacks rather than mundane day to day matters.

(c)  Courts Martial Papers for trials during WWI were destroyed in the 1940 bombing. The exceptions are those for men who were executed, these are open for inspection but have now been requisitioned back to the Ministry of Defence. However, lists giving names appear in WO93/49 (death sentences carried out in the British Army during WWI), WO93/42-45 (nominal rolls of courts martial of all ranks of Australian and Canadian forces 1915-19), WO86, WO88, WO90, WO92 and WO213. *See* TNA Leaflet No.84 *Records of Courts Martial; Army*.

(d)  Embarkation lists — may exist for zones other than France but even then only likely to mention officer i/c draft.

(e)  Casualty return slips or counterfoils. Admission books for a few military medical units survive at TNA Kew in MH106.

(f)  Lists of Prisoners of War.

There are no lists of prisoners of war in TNA at Kew (*see* TNA Leaflet No 72). Some may be mentioned in correspondence regarding prisoners in FO 383 and CO 537/1123 (the latter covers British prisoners in Turkey). The International Red Cross in Geneva keeps lists of prisoners and internees for the war. They are housed in the International Red Cross Library in Geneva and there is currently no public access or enquiry service. (*see* The Central Tracing Agency of the International Committee of the Red Cross, C.R. Chapman, in *Family Tree Magazine*, Vol. 10, No. 7 (May), 1994.

# 3. FAMILY RECORDS

As in any genealogical research project, the first task is to gather together all the available family documents and oral data on the ancestor. These are likely to include photographs, letters, medals and perhaps the occasional official document such as a discharge certificate. Shortly after the war started it became an offence, even for officers, to have cameras or to keep diaries. However, the large numbers of books and collections of personal diaries in the Imperial War Museum Library give hope that many men disobeyed both orders.

Both in England and on the Continent many professional photographers made a living taking photographs of single soldiers or of groups, so most men were able to send pictures of themselves in uniform back to their loved ones in England. Although these were endorsed *Somewhere in France* they usually carry a date. By careful examination of the photographs and with the help of a guide, you should be able to determine, from the various buttons and badges, the regiment or corps to which your ancestor belonged. Years of service can be estimated from service and good conduct stripes. Postmarks will enable the dates of embarkation to be tied down as closely as possible, i.e. between the last letter posted in England and the first in France. With luck (and most research depends at sometime or other on luck) you may find a photo taken after the war when censorship was ended. This will give a date and a positive location. Letters sent to the soldier are also valuable. They often give the unit of the ancestor in the address. Read all the letters and cards to obtain any clue.

What you are trying to obtain is information on:
- Dates (can they be deduced from the contents or postmarks?).
- Postings and locations.
- Name of unit (regiment, corps and, if possible, the battalion or unit number).
- Medals (is he wearing medal ribbons or do you have them?).
- His army number (may be on the medal or a letter).
- Years of service (from dates and service stripes).
- Type of work (for instance the background to a picture might show a stable or workshop).

Don't forget to look at his companions - if it is a group photo, the badges and insignia may be clearer in the front row.

The next move is to check the photos with the pictures of badges and other insignia as shown in the various reference books (*see* Bibliography and, in particular, *Companion Volumes* Ref. 2 and Refs. 36, 38 and 62). Do not be surprised if the badges show a different unit to that given by other sources. It was not uncommon for men to transfer, or be transferred to, other units. In 1917 for instance, many men were taken out of the Army Service Corps and transferred to front line infantry units. Wounded men who recovered, but were reckoned unfit for the rigours of life in the trenches, were almost invariably transferred to the Labour Corps for work behind the lines, as were elderly men.

At this point, it would be as well to search for the name in the National Roll of Honour (*see* Bibliography Ref. 33) but copies may be difficult to locate. This lists men who served not just those who died. Some libraries have the volumes that cover their own town. If it is known that the ancestor died in action, then a search should firstly be made in the Miscellaneous Section of the Records of Births, Marriages and Deaths at the Family Records Centre. (*see* Bibliography Ref. 5).

Details of his regiment, place of enlistment and sometimes residence can be found in *Soldiers Died in the Great War* (*see* Bibliography Ref. 32) but this is arranged by regiment. If you don't know his regiment, it is easier to consult the CD Rom, now widely available in record offices and family history society libraries. This is arranged alphabetically for the whole of the Army and includes Officers. Similar details are available from the Commonwealth War Graves Commission Cemetery lists (*see* Bibliography Ref. 34) which also gives the next of kin and this is now available online at www.cwgc.org.

Remember that the numbers involved are very high and even rare surnames can be found with identical forenames in different regiments. Make sure you have found the right one. It is safer to search the lot unless you are 100% sure.

Family tradition or oral information should not be neglected. The tales passed down may recall a particular town or battle - even the address of a French girlfriend may provide evidence of a period of time spent in a certain village. Tradition may also give the name of a regiment or type of work. 'He drove lorries full of shells' or 'I spent the war filling in leave permits and never got one for myself' or 'Major Blenkinsop, my old CO, would never have allowed it'. Such remarks provide a good clue that can be followed up but do not be fooled by mention of Ypres or the Somme. There were four battles of Ypres and only two of the 50 plus Divisions did **not** fight on the Somme.

There are a number of items the family may still have. If your ancestor was wounded or fell sick and discharged he would have been sent a silver badge inscribed *For King and Empire: Services Rendered*. If he died, then as well as a telegram and a letter from his CO, the next of kin were sent a 4¼" diameter brass plaque with his name engraved on it. The design of the plaque was based on the winning entry of a competition held in 1919. It depicts a figure of Britannia and a lion. The plaques were issued in 1919 in cardboard containers within a white envelope bearing the Royal Crest. In a separate cardboard roll each recipient also had an 11" x 7" scroll recording that the soldier died *that others might live in freedom* and giving his rank, name and regiment. Also enclosed was a letter from the King. (For a full account *see Swinnerton Family History Journal*, No 4, January 1980). Those who have one of the plaques might be interested to know that the late Miss Rose E.B. Coombs of the Imperial War Museum prepared an unpublished paper on the subject which gives a great deal of detail, including references to *The Times* concerning the competition.

For Christmas 1914 all members of the British Expeditionary Force received a card from the King. This was inscribed *May God protect you and bring you home safe*. In 1915 all wounded men in hospital received a similar card.

If you still have your ancestor's medals, these will give positive details of his regiment or corps, number, rank and name (engraved round the rim or on the back), but not his unit or battalions except on the 1914 Star. The three most common were nicknamed Pip, Squeak and Wilfred after three characters in a newspaper cartoon. More correctly, they are the '1914 Star' (often erroneously called the 'Mons Star'), the 'British War Medal' and the 'Victory Medal'.

**The 1914 star** was a bronze four-pointed star behind crossed swords, superimposed with a crowned wreath. A central scroll is inscribed *1914*. This was given to officers and men who served with a unit in France or Belgium between 5th August 1914 and midnight on 22nd/23rd November 1914. A bar bearing the words *5 Aug-22 Nov '14* was added to the ribbon for those who had served under the fire of the enemy between these dates. When the ribbon only was worn a small rosette was added to this ribbon to indicate the 'under fire' bar.

**A 1914 -15 Star** was also issued which was identical in design except that the wording on the central scroll reads '1914-15'. This was for those who served from 23 November 1914 to 31st December 1915 in France and Belgium but did not have the 1914 Star and those who served in any other theatre of war between 5th August 1914 and 31st December 1915.

**The British War Medal** is silver and bears an effigy of the King on the face and St. George on horseback on the reverse. It was awarded to those personnel who entered a theatre of war or served overseas in other officially approved areas between 5 August 1914 and 11th November 1918. This was later extended to include service in Russia 1919-1920.

**The Victory Medal** is bronze and shows a winged figure of Victory. It was given to personnel who served overseas in a theatre of war for a period between 5th August 1914 and 11th November 1918. The ribbon can carry a small bronze oak leaf denoting one or more *Mentions in Despatches*.

**The Territorial Force Medal** in bronze was awarded to all men who had been members of the Territorial Force on 30th September 1914 and who subsequently served in a theatre of war but did not qualify for the 1914 or 1914-15 Star.

If you find that your ancestor was awarded a gallantry medal or was mentioned in despatches, check the entry in the *London Gazette*. This was issued daily and included long supplements of medal recipients and those mentioned in despatches. The lists were usually arranged in alphabetical order within regiments and corps. If you do not know which one, it takes a long time to search. The issues containing lists can be located in the quarterly indexes. After 1916, individual names of recipients as well as the issue number are given in the indexes.

Look under *State Intelligence - War Office*. Sets of the *London Gazette* can be found in a few of the larger libraries but some do not have an index. The Guildhall Library has a complete set and the indexes are on open shelves. A similar set is in The National Archives at Kew, look in Class Z, together with index volumes for the war years which are on open shelves in the Microfilm Room. When calling for the required bound monthly volume, take care - the index does not give the volume number, only page numbers which run right through a year's issues (12 volumes). The counter staff have a conversion list - page number to month, and hence volume for each year.

The Gazette is now also available on the internet at www.gazettes-online.co.uk.

# 4. MEDAL ROLLS AT THE NATIONAL ARCHIVES, KEW

The Medal Rolls, which were at one time at the Army Medal Office at Droitwich, have now been transferred to The National Archives at Kew. There are a number of leaflets which researchers will find of use.

*No. 101, Service Medals and Award Rolls, War of 1914 18.*
This covers the use of records dealing with service medals. These are the British War Medal, Victory Medal, 1914 Star, 1914 -1915 Star, Territorial Force War Medal and the Silver War Badge (for soldiers discharged wounded or sick). The records and the indexes to which the leaflet refers are for officers and other ranks in the army and the Royal Flying Corps and form part of Classes WO329 and WO372.

*No. 105, First World War; Indexes to Medal Entitlement.*
This covers the Distinguished Conduct Medal (DCM), Meritorious Service Medal (MSM), Military Medal (MM) and Mentions in Despatches. It also has information regarding the *London Gazette*.

*No. 108, Records of Medals.*
This is a more general leaflet which covers all medals, for all services, for all periods. It has a list of TNA class numbers for medal rolls.

The indexes to service medals, as described in leaflet No. 101, are on 25,000 microfiche housed in small filing cabinets on a table in the centre of the Microfilm Reading Room. They have the class number WO372. You select a viewer and take the numbered dummy fiche from your viewer to the cabinets, locate the required fiche and replace it with the dummy. After viewing the fiche, return it to the correct place, marked by your dummy. Take only one fiche at a time to be fair to other researchers. The fiche collection contains images of about 9 million index cards, usually one per soldier.

The arrangement of the cards on the fiche is not straightforward. Each fiche has six rows each of 12 frames. Each frame shows six index cards arranged as follows: at the left-hand side of the frame, three cards one under the other in the order 1, 2, 3 with 1 at the top. On the right-hand side of the frame, three cards one under the other in the order 4, 5, 6. Thus No. 4 is at the top of the frame. Therefore to search in sequence one must move along the top row of frames whilst moving down and up each column of three in turn. The names are in strict alphabetical order of surnames although the usual warning of mis-spelling and misfiling always applies in addition to uncertainties of the position of 'Mac' or 'Mc' and of hyphenated surnames.

Within each surname there are several alphabetical sequences, the first for single initials followed by that for one Christian name. Then comes one name plus one initial, followed by two Christian names and lastly three Christian names, e.g. first comes SMITH, A. to SMITH, Z.; followed by SMITH, Abel to SMITH, Zack; then SMITH, Adam A. to SMITH, Zack Z. and finally SMITH, Arthur, A.A. to SMITH, Zack Z.Z. This means that, with common surnames, three or more sequences must be searched to ensure that the correct card is found. As it is well known that some people did not always use their full set of given names, all sequences should be searched anyway. Should two or more soldiers have the same names, they are listed in order of regimental seniority (*see* Appendix 1).

The index cards show name, regiment, rank and service number. This is usually only the regiment or corps but sometimes also gives details of the battalion, battery or other unit. Against each listed medal a code number leads the researcher to the roll containing the record of issue of the medal. Using the finding aid (WO329/1) on a table in the Microfilm Reading Room, the code number can be converted to TNA reference number in Class WO329. Photocopies of the record cards can be obtained. A further code gives the **Operational Theatres of War** for which the medal was awarded. A list of these codes is given in *Army Service Records of the First World War* by William Spencer, published by The National Archives, Kew (*see* Bibliography Ref.14). The rolls rarely give any more details than those given on the index cards. The dates listed on the cards for the 1914 Star and the 1914-1915 Star should show when the recipient first entered the operational theatres of war to qualify for the medal but do not always do so. The date given in the roll for the Silver War Badge is the date the recipient joined the army, which is not necessarily the same date as that on which he joined the unit from which he was discharged. Some cards and/or ledgers also give the date of discharge or death. The rolls of the Silver War Badges give the date and cause of discharge (whether through sickness or from wounds) and the age at discharge.

# 5. SOLDIERS' PERSONAL SERVICE RECORDS

The total number of men and women in the United Kingdom in uniform for at least some time during the war was about 5,060,000 or some 11% of the total population of 46,000,000. Of these, 47% or 2,377,876 became casualties. This number includes men who were wounded several times, so perhaps is a little on the high side. Deaths were 744,000 or nearly 9% of the male population aged between 25 and 40.

In common with soldiers from 1760 onwards, those who served in the First World War had a personnel file recording their complete army service.

Microfilm copies of service records for other ranks whose service ended between 1914 and 1920 have now been transferred from the custody of the Ministry of Defence to the Public Record Office, Kew. **The actual documents, however, remain at the MOD Depot at Glasgow.**

The records were originally kept so that the War Office (as it then was) could answer queries about pensions, medals and allowances for disablement. Sadly, during the last war about 60% of them were destroyed in the bombing of an army warehouse in London. Most of those that survived were badly damaged either by fire or from the water that was used to put out the flames. They have become known as the *Burnt Collection* and contain the service records of roughly 25-30% of the estimated 5 million men who served in the British Army in the Great War. They are stored in a staggering 33,000 boxes on nearly 2 miles of shelving but are in such a fragile condition that **they will never be open to public inspection.**

The National Archives received a grant from the Lottery Fund to finance a project to conserve and microfilm them. They have all now been filmed and the films are available for inspection.. They are classified as WO 363 but in many cases, only fragments of pages have survived.

There is another collection of records known as *the Unburnt Collection.* This is also available for searching. These were compiled from duplicate records held by the Ministry of Pensions and comprise the records of another 8-10% of the soldiers. These have been microfilmed by the Genealogical Society of Utah and were released for public consumption at a special conference held at TNA on Armistice Day 1996. It is hoped to have copies of these in other locations in due course and they are, of course, available through LDS Family History Libraries. They have been classified as WO 364.

The files in Class WO364 contain records of men and women who fall into a number of classes. It is unlikely that those who died during the war without having dependants to whom a pension could be paid are included, nor are those who were discharged at the end of the war without a pension. Most of the records concern men who were pre-war soldiers who had been discharged on completion of service before 1920 or records of men who were discharged on medical grounds before 1920 and who had joined before or after 1914. They need not have had any overseas service. The records of some pre-war soldiers who rejoined in 1914 and were then discharged during the war are known to have been filed in the last batch (1883 - 1913) of Soldiers' Papers in WO97.

A personal inspection for names from the author's own family revealed an increase of about 25% in the number known to have served, many of whom were, in fact, discharged through ill health, some after only a few weeks in the Army. The medical reports on these men revealed medical conditions so obvious that one wonders how they were accepted in the first place.

In preparation for the release of the film of the Unburnt Documents in November 1996, Lesley Wynne-Davis and her team from the Friends of the Public Record Office conducted a survey of the documents then held at Hayes. A search for the records of soldiers listed in the medal rolls in both the Unburnt and Burnt Documents revealed papers for between 20% and 33% of those in the medal rolls. The rest must be considered to have been destroyed in the bombing. In each case, papers for a few additional soldiers, not mentioned in the medal rolls, can be found among the Unburnt Documents in WO364. The lost documents appeared to be distributed among all regiments and corps and no one group appears to have suffered from being nearest to the bomb's impact. Although the records are now in strict alphabetical order, they were known, at one time, to have been arranged in order of seniority of regiments. This can be confirmed by a few filing mistakes. On the whole, however, little is known of the history of the documents and there is much uncertainty about the filing system. Further details of these 1914 -18 Soldiers' Papers can be found in TNA book on the subject. (*see* Bibliography Ref. 14.)

Both the Burnt and Unburnt Collections include service records not only for regular soldiers (which can date back to the 1880s) but also for members of the Territorial Force and Special Reserve who had enlisted pre-war and for members of the Royal Flying Corps.

Official lists of wounded were issued at frequent intervals by the Deputy Adjutant General's Office. Some of these lists were published in part in *The Times*, and extracts appeared in local newspapers. From August 1917 the list appeared weekly and a set has been preserved in the Newspaper Library, Colindale, London. It is not indexed and a search for one man means a search of the whole volume, day after day for every type of casualty. There is no known example of the pre-August 1917 daily lists.

# 6. ARMY ORGANISATION

It will help if you make yourself familiar with the general organisation of our armies in France so that you can get an overall picture. Without this, you will not be able to locate those records that still remain. (Figs. 4 -7.)

You should by now be in the position of knowing if your ancestor was in a corps or a regiment and as the method of further search depends to a certain extent on which type of unit he was in, you should understand the main differences.

## Regiment

This can be of infantry who fought on foot  or cavalry who fought on horseback . The regiment is the traditional fighting unit with names such as the King's Own Yorkshire Light Infantry, the Worcestershire Regiment or 14th Hussars.  A list is provided in Appendix I.  An infantry regiment usually had two battalions during peace time; each of approximately 1,000 men plus, in most cases, a Militia battalion and one or more Territorial Force battalions. These Territorials were part time soldiers who trained with the regiment in their spare time for a retainer.  The 1st Battalion of a regiment was frequently stationed overseas to help keep the flag flying over the Empire while the 2nd Battalion remained at home to train new recruits. Each regiment had a depot or HQ in a town associated with it, such as the county town.

With the outbreak of war, the number of recruits increased manyfold and extra battalions were formed.  At the same time the Territorials were called to full time service.  A regiment could often have more than 10 battalions and these, although they bore the regiment's name and wore its insignia, were allocated throughout the army as separate independent units. The 1st and 2nd Battalions might serve in France while the 5th Battalion was in Egypt. It is thus important to know with which battalions the ancestor served. The battalions were identified by a number which can take several forms.

1st Mummersets
(this means the 1st Battalion of the Mummerset Regiment.

5th Mummersets
(this means the 5th Battalion of the Mummerset Regiment, which was usually a Territorial Force Battalion.)

1/5thMummersets
(this means the First Line Battalion of the 5th Territorial Battalion of the Mummerset Regiment. It was renamed from the 5th Battalion a few days after the start of the war.)

2/5th Mummersets
(this means the 2nd Line Battalion of the 5th Territorial Battalion. It was formed to take on new recruits and those men who did not volunteer for overseas service at the outbreak of war.)

10th Mummersets
(one of the many new battalions formed during the war.)

An infantry regiment thus consisted of a number of battalions each of around 1,000 men. The soldiers in a regiment were, in nearly all cases, fighting soldiers. Included in the nominal number of 1,000, however, were a number of non-fighting personnel who nevertheless were still members of the battalions. They could include:

Stretcher-bearers - up to 32 when going into battle.

Cooks.

Bandsmen who usually doubled as additional stretcher- bearers.

Batmen (officers' servants)

Transport Drivers. Each battalion had to provide men for its collection of hand carts and horse-drawn wagons which carried kit, tents and other equipment.

This reduced the fighting strength to about 800 men. Some battalions, usually of low medical grade men, were stationed for general duties in depots and HQs. Others had the suffix '(Labour)' or '(Pioneer)'and were used for behind-the-line labouring jobs in addition to the Labour Corps formed in 1914 especially for that purpose.

The infantry battalion was made up of a number of *Companies* (usually four plus a Headquarters Company). They were normally commanded by a Captain with a Company Sgt Major as the senior NCO. Each company was made up of four *Platoons* commanded by a Lieutenant or 2nd/Lieutenant with a Sergeant to assist him and a Corporal as the Sergeant's deputy. Each platoon consisted of three *Sections* in charge of a Lance Corporal. Whilst you may well find your ancestor's address as 'B Coy, 2nd Battalion, the section number was never used in addresses. However, due to the very high casualty rates, companies were often commanded by junior officers and platoons by NCOs.

A company could also be a unit of a named corps working as a group, e.g. No. 24 Motor Ambulance Convoy (645 Coy ASC).

In a cavalry regiment the companies were called *Squadrons* and the platoons *Troops.* A regiment of cavalry had about 500 men divided into three squadrons each of four troops. The troops of about 40 men were split into sections. There were 28 regiments of cavalry - 7 of Dragoon Guards and 21 of Dragoons, Hussars and Lancers. There were also numerous regiments of Territorial Force cavalry called Yeomanry - *see* Appendix 1.

## Brigade

Normally the sub-division of a division, numbered from 1 upwards e.g. 1st and 2nd Brigades but artillery regiments were also called brigades -see later. An infantry brigade consisted of four battalions (reduced to three in 1918.) Each numbered brigade was allocated to a numbered division, usually on a permanent basis at a rate of three brigades per division. A few brigades were named, e.g. The Guards Brigade made up solely of the regiments of Foot Guards.

Each division had four brigades of artillery attached to it, each brigade having four batteries of four guns each. This meant that the total fire power was 64 guns although the number changed many times during the war. These artillery brigades were numbered in Roman numerals (as opposed to normal figures for brigades of infantry) and the numbering sequence ran through the whole of the other forces, not just the division to which they were attached. Numbers in the hundreds were common, e.g. CCXXIII. The batteries within each brigade were numbered A, B, C, D for Horse and 1, 2, 3, 4 for Field, Siege, Heavy and Mountain Artillery. During the war the artillery arrangements were changed many times and the footnotes in *Becke (see* Bibliography Ref.31) must be studied to find the movements of each battery. In the later years of the war many of the heavier batteries were attached to corps or armies, not to divisions.

## Division

Divisions were the smallest completely self-contained fighting organisation — they had their own infantry, artillery and support services. The units in them tended to be kept together without change throughout the war whereas the allocation of divisions to army corps (and army corps to armies) was frequently changed to meet the needs of battle.

A division was composed of three brigades. The total strength of a division in 1914-18 was about 18,000 men, 4000 horses and 850 wagons. There were over 70 such divisions which were numbered 1st, 2nd, etc. up to 71st plus three cavalry divisions (1st, 2nd and 3rd). A few divisions also had names, e.g. 51st (Highland) Division. Appendix II gives a list of divisional numbers and names

Each division had its own supporting troops called **Divisional Troops** who were not, as their name would suggest, men who make up a division but units usually of an auxiliary (signals, transport, clerks, medical, etc.) nature reporting directly to and supporting the headquarters of the division..

Within a division, battalions sometimes had names besides the normal number. In the 41st Division, for example, the 122nd Infantry Brigade consisted of four battalions named Bermondsey (12th East Surrey Regiment), 2nd Portsmouth (15th Hampshire Regiment), Lewisham (11th Queen's Own Royal West Kent Regiment) and Arts and Crafts (18th King's Royal Rifle Corps).

In the same division the field artillery brigades bore similar type names, the CLXXXIII Brigade being named Hampstead and the divisional ammunition column, the West Ham. The names often denoted that the men enlisted in a town as the result of recruiting drives. Careful reading of the many footnotes in Becke will trace most names. (*See* extracts in Figs. 6 and 7).

## Corps

The word 'corps' is used with three different meanings. This can be very confusing for the non-military minded ancestor researcher. In this current context, the word means a large unit of specialised troops. Examples would be the Royal Army Medical Corps, Army Service Corps and the Corps of Royal Engineers (RE), each of which would have many sub-units.

Note that the Artillery (usually known as just the Royal Artillery (RA) but correctly entitled the Royal Regiment of Artillery) is not strictly speaking a Corps but presents the same problems to the researcher because it was divided into a large number of artillery brigades - *see* above.

The corps were far larger than the regiments - the Army Service Corps (ASC) for instance had over 300,000 men and they were not associated with a particular town or county. At the Corps HQ, men would be trained in the skills appropriate to the corps and then assembled into self-contained units to carry out a particular function. Because of the need for skilled men the pay was several times that of the infantry soldier. On the other hand, the medical standards of the individuals were frequently lower.

Each corps would have many types of unit for carrying out the multitude of tasks necessary to keep an army in fighting condition. The ASC had over 10 types of unit involved with transport alone. A list of some of the more common corps unit types is given in Appendix III. The size of the units depended on their function and was laid down in their war establishment (page 32, q.v.) but in general was far smaller than that of an infantry battalion. In 1915, for example, a Field Ambulance Workshop - an Army Service Corps unit - consisted of only 20 men.

Some units could be even smaller. As an added complication some men were 'attached' to a unit of another corps but had no unit number of their own. Thus the establishment of a Field Ambulance, a Royal Army Medical Corps (RAMC) unit of some 200 men, included 45 ASC personnel. This meant that the number of units in a corps was far higher than the number of battalions in a regiment. Moreover, it was not usual to give the name or number of the unit in the various sources mentioned so far, so the family historian has a problem.

With regiments, the task is to identify, with the aid of regimental histories, the ancestor's battalion out of, perhaps, 10 such units. This can usually be done fairly easily from books that are available in the local library. With corps, the number of units could run to over a thousand, involving perhaps 100 different types, and as the histories of corps units are very specialised, they are hard to come by nor do they often mention specific units by name or number.

When dealing with men who served with one of the corps and not knowing the unit number, the search can be very long indeed. Even when a unit has been identified there is only a slim chance of proving that the correct one has been found.

## Army Corps

An army corps, not to be confused with the corps above, was a fighting organisation consisting of four to six divisions plus the usual service troops called Army Corps Troops (see Bibliography Ref.63). The word 'army' is usually omitted thus adding to the confusion. 'Army Corps' for example, was usually written in the form XXI Corps.

## Armies

Directly under the command of the General Headquarters (GHQ) were the 5 armies. These armies were formed at different times and the numbers given to each also changed. GHQ also had control of a number of 'Lines of Communication Troops' who were often corps units which provided the basic services for the armies - depots, transport, base hospitals etc. (*see* examples in Appendix III). At various times some of these units would be allocated by GHQ to one of the armies on a temporary basis and they would thus report to that army's HQ instead of GHQ.

Each army also had its own army troops and also some special fighting troops, such as heavy artillery and tanks whose disposition was placed at the disposal of the HQ rather than the next lower echelon of command. They tended to be permanently attached to the HQ although the lower echelons were often changed. Often included also was a company of soldiers for general 'odd jobs' to provide basic services for that army. They did, however, include one or more battalions of infantry, usually made up of low medical grade men for general duties around the HQ including the defence of the headquarters. Once again the commander of the army could allocate some of his army troops to report directly to the next echelon down. An army had three or four army corps of fighting men or roughly three or four times 80,000 men, say 250,000 -300,000 per army.

## Other units

**HQ Troops** - The troops needed to run the GHQ plus some corps units held as a general reserve.

**Lines of Communication Troops** - units under the direct control of GHQ, mainly connected with supply, etc. but not necessarily so, which provided a service for the whole of the British Forces in France.

**Park** - A place where ammunition, supplies and vehicles were stored together with the lorries which transported them. Also, the name of the type of unit that manned the lorries, e.g. an Ammunition Supply Park was an ASC unit that arranged the transport and storage of ammunition for a corps.

**Field Ambulance** - a unit (not just a vehicle) comprising both Army Service Corps and Royal Army Medical Corps men who manned a first aid post and drove motor and horse ambulances.

**Convoy** - a line of vehicles on the move and also the unit that manned the vehicles and serviced them.

**Cadre** - or 'to reduce to a cadre'. If a unit suffered heavy losses or was to be reorganised, it was often reduced to a few officers and men to keep the name on the books until it was re-formed with new men. With infantry battalions it usually meant a reduction to 10 officers and 45 other ranks (normal strength about 1,000 total), the surplus being sent to a base depot for re-allocation although the Engineers, Artillery, etc. were often re-allocated within the immediate area.

# 7. ORDERS OF BATTLE AND ALLOCATIONS

These terms are used for the books and documents which give the organisation of the Army at any particular point in the war. This is a sort of family tree of the Army and, just as we draw our trees in several forms, the Army also has many methods of describing who reports to whom.

There appear to be five general sources, of which only one, Becke can be obtained through the inter-library loan service. Part of the *Official History*, Becke sets out which armies, army corps and divisions took part in each of the battles of the war. Each of the 70-odd divisions is broken down into the battalions and divisional troops (i.e. the Artillery (RA), Engineers (RE), ASC and RAMC units) which fought with the divisions. The footnotes enable the researcher to trace the activities of both battalions and divisional troops within a division during the course of the war. It does not cover L of C, army, or corps troops.

In The National Archives Reference Room there is a copy of Brig. E.A. James's book giving details of each regiment (*see* Bibliography Ref.15). The Imperial War Museum Printed Books Library also has a copy.

TNA at Kew has a set of the orders of battle issued by GHQ in France. These are arranged in a different manner to Becke. Each refers to the situation at a specific date, usually at approximately monthly intervals. It gives lists of all GHQ, L of C, army and corps troops as well as the divisions with which each battalion fought at that date. It has tables that give the allocation of each unit of the corps (ASC, RE, RAMC) as well as artillery. As these allocations changed often during the war, the whole set has to be searched to ensure that a true picture has been obtained.

The allocation lists were also issued as separate publications for each corps and some of these can be found in TNA and at some regimental museums.

ASC Allocations WO33/730/744/893.

Army Troops Allocations WO33/829/827.

Other allocation lists, including the ASC, RA and RAMC, can be found in WO95/5494. Part of the RAMC allocations can be found in Vol 3 of *Medical History of the Great War* (*see* Bibliography Ref.26).

The contents of WO95/5494 are:

Folder A - Allocation of Siege Batteries

Folder B - Allocation of Canadian Siege Batteries

Folder C - Allocation of Heavy Artillery Batteries

Folder D - Allocation of Royal Horse and Royal Field Artillery Batteries, two volumes

Folder E - Allocation of ASC units of all types with note of war diary number

Folder F - Allocation of ASC units Motor Transport and Horse Transport only

Folder G - Allocation of ASC Motor Transport

Folder H - Index to RASC units

Folder I - Allocation of Machine Gun Companies

Folder J - Allocation of Entrenching Battalions

Folder K - Allocation of Medical Units

Folder L - Allocation of RAMC Locations

Order of Battle of British Army in France General Staff GHQ.
Imperial War Museum Library. TNA Kew also has what is believed to be a complete set under the following reference numbers.

WO95/5467 France 1914-16

WO95/5468 France 1916-17

WO95/5469 France 1918

WO95/5470 Rhine Army 1919

Other neighbouring sequences cover the Home Army and other war zones. *See* also

WO33/911 Russia ⎫
WO33/795 Home Divisions ⎬ These are possibly duplicates of the WO95 series.
WO33/829 Army Troops ⎭

Lastly, the index to war diaries WO95 on the shelves of the reference room at Kew, is in the form of an Order of Battle for October 1918.

Although these sources were republished at intervals, they were not always correct. As an example, the basic unit of ASC transport was the company. This was attached to a division to carry supplies from the railhead or other dump up to the divisional supply point. Its full name, as obtained from an allocation list, might be 'No. 179 Coy ASC (18th Div. Supply Column)'. However, the history of No. 179 Coy ASC, written by the

Company Sergeant Major, says that when the 18th Division moved to another part of the front in 1916, the supply column stayed behind and acted as supply column for the 34th Div. which took over the front vacated by the 18th. The name of the company, however, remained the '18th Div. Supply Column' until 1917 when it was changed to '34th Div. Transport Column' as part of a reorganisation of army transport. Such changes are only partly apparent from a study of the allocation lists and orders of battle.

In general, each division, its brigades and battalions together with the divisional troops stayed together throughout the war. However, there were enough exceptions to prevent the researcher basing too many assumptions on this apparent permanency. The following are a few examples.

- The 30th - 35th Divisions were disbanded in April 1915 but later reformed. The rearrangement of the Army in April 1915, which meant the disbanding and re-forming of a number of divisions, is covered in great detail in the Appendix to Vol 3b of Becke.

- In March 1918 the four battalions of each brigade were reduced to three. This meant that men were transferred to other battalions or brigades. Becke gives details of these moves in many footnotes.

- Movements of the Royal Artillery brigades were very complicated. They were constantly changed with the introduction of new guns and manning arrangements; again Becke gives helpful information.

- In March 1916 the Field Ambulance Workshops (ASC units) were absorbed into the Divisional Supply Column. This latter unit, also of the ASC, was part of the corps troops but allocated by the corps to the division. Many divisions lost their cavalry and cyclist companies in 1916 and acquired machine gun companies in 1917.

The researcher dealing with a difficult case must be prepared to study changes and movements such as the above in great detail if he is to achieve the desired result.

# 8. MONTHLY RETURNS

If you have managed to tie the embarkation for France down to a month or two from dated letters, cards, etc., then the monthly returns in TNA will help you trace the ancestor's unit. These returns show where the units of the army were stationed each month. For home-based units, the town or training depot is given but for the others only the single word *Overseas* or *France* is used. The date when the unit was first posted to the current location is given for home-based units only.

In the Overseas section there are often two groups of units, one smaller group will be those units outside Europe, while the other, usually larger, will be marked 'B.E.F.' and refers to France. Lists of exact sailing dates for some corps units are given in WO95/5494.

An examination of the actual date for leaving the UK for those units listed for the first time in the Overseas section, shows that they had all sailed by the middle of the previous month, i.e. the June issue did not include units which were sent overseas after about the 15th of May. However, some returns took a long time to appear in print and the same June issue might well include for the first time units who sailed for France before the 15th April and who would normally have been included in the May issue.

By carefully checking through these books, which are bound in 4-monthly volumes, it is possible to estimate the date when your ancestor left the UK and also to trace his movements within the UK. This latter point is most important, as war diaries do not, in general, start until the unit arrives on a foreign shore. On this point, some of the divisional histories given in Becke provide further information on UK service but even he had difficulty in finding data for the production of his volume.

For those who still cannot positively identify the exact unit, the date of sailing of several possible units could be compared with known dates from family sources. When the number of possible units has been reduced to a manageable quantity, the war diaries of these possible units can be examined to reduce the numbers still further. The benefit of the monthly returns, as opposed to other sources, is that the entries are listed by month and by type of unit. It is thus possible to cover several different types of unit with the minimum of search time. A further list of embarkation dates for various units is given in WO 162/7 in TNA at Kew.

The general monthly returns of the regimental strength of the British Army have their own class at Kew. WO73/97-111 covers WWI. WO73/102 covers Jan-April 1916. WO33/763 and WO25/3548 also give lists of troop ship sailings to destinations other than France. Some of the lists in WO95/5494 give exact sailing dates of units.

WO162/7 is a manuscript list of embarkation dates, the arrangement of which is difficult to understand. Use with care. It does include some of the more unusual units. The main embarkation series is WO25/3535 et seq.

# 9. WAR DIARIES

Every unit of battalion size or greater kept a war diary. The same applies to smaller but self-contained units of the various corps. Even the Field Ambulance Workshops with a strength of only 20 men kept a war diary. These are available in TNA at Kew in WO 95/1 to over 5,494.

If the unit cannot be found easily in the Class Index then WO95/5494 contains a miscellaneous collection of allocation lists for several corps. These are notated with the war diary piece number in several cases. Other notes index units of several corps against the location in which they served and give the date of sailing. War diaries of home-based units are to be found in the index around WO95/5455.

The class list for war diaries is in three binders under 'WO95'. The second and third binders list the units according to the Order of Battle 1918. This is not the most helpful of arrangements but the first binder has an index for infantry battalions and for artillery brigades. For other non-infantry units there is a separate manuscript index in a red binder in the Reference Room - Additional Finding Aids, classes J - WO. The index gives dates for some units. War diaries did not usually start until arrival on foreign soil whereas other records give a date for leaving the UK. For France this might not be important but for other war zones, the difference in dates could be significant. With the supporting troops the method of indexing makes the search for a particular unit rather time-consuming. It is worth searching WO95/5494 as this has an index by unit number for some corps. Be warned that some units, due to mergers, may have two or more diaries kept in different boxes.

A day's entry could be a single word, e.g. 'Training', or a full page of tightly packed handwritten script detailing the movement of the unit to a new location with full details of the billets, messing and state of the weather. An action could take many pages. Be warned, however, that the names of individual private soldiers seldom appear. Gallantry awards often rate a mention as do unusual offences even if not followed by a court martial. NCOs appear more often whilst practically every officer is named once or twice. It has been noted that some army staff diaries give an official weather report. (2nd Army Director of Medical Services WO95/285.)

Careful reading of the ancestor's unit diary is worthwhile for although his name is unlikely to be there, a great deal of background is to be found in its pages. Even information of a true family history nature can be found. One such entry reports that the officer in charge was on special leave to Ireland to visit his sick mother and another reports the transfer of a man to another unit nearby so that he could be with his brother. In both cases, names were given, which is rare in the case of other ranks.

Even less likely to give names are the military HQ papers for armies, corps and divisions in WO158 which usually deal with plans for large scale actions.

As war diaries are the only remaining contemporary source available to the majority of searchers, every effort should be made to extract all the information from them. Not only should the diary of the ancestor's unit be carefully read but also those of the next echelon up in the army organisation. If the unit was a battalion, then check the brigade and divisional diaries; if a corps unit, search the diary of the responsible staff officer at brigade, divisional or corps HQ. It is also rewarding to examine the diaries of those units who performed their duties in conjunction with the ancestor's unit or who trained or travelled together.

The ancestor's unit, a Motor Ambulance Convoy, arrived in France and was stationed at a small village. The war diary does not give a precise map reference or details of the billet. However, there is an indirect mention of tents. The diary of the Deputy Director of Medical Services at Corps HQ to whom the unit reported states that the DDMS visited the site of the MAC giving a map reference and adding that the tents, being pitched in a wood, could not be arranged in a neat military manner. At a later date after a change of location the DDMS reports a visit from the officer in charge of the MAC who complains that his men had been turned out of their billets to make room for an infantry battalion and that they now had insufficient tentage. The DDMS was able to arrange for the supply of 15 rolls of (tarred) felting and wood to construct huts as well as making two bell tents available. No mention was made of these events in the unit's own diary.

On another occasion, the war diary reports that two ambulances were lost when the enemy overran the advanced dressing station run by No.36 Field Ambulance (a medical unit, not a vehicle). This is confirmed by a brief description of the event in the official *Medical History*. The official *Military History* also refers to the incident and reports the fall of the village by 8.30 am on 30th November 1917 but makes no reference to medical units.

A search of the diary of No. 36 Field Ambulance reveals that the pages for November 1917 are missing (were they lost in the action?) but also filed most thoughtfully in the same box is a copy of the history of the field ambulance prepared by the unit historian a few months later. This devotes an entire page to the action and tells how some of the men escaped.

War diaries of artillery units are reported to be less helpful. Only artillery brigades kept diaries, not the individual batteries, and these tended only to give the location of Brigade HQ and not the location of the guns. The remoteness of the batteries from Brigade HQ also precluded any mention of individual men. Frequent changes of location, often at night, was another reason given for poor diaries. None of this makes the task of the researcher any easier when dealing with the constant change of brigade composition.

# 10. WAR ESTABLISHMENTS

The war establishment is a document which gives the number of men supposed to be in a unit with details of the principal equipment, e.g. guns or lorries.

Some are given in Miscellaneous War Office Papers in TNA Kew. WO33/743/778/900-902/789 and it is believed a complete set is in WO23/900 - et seq. Others may be found in regimental museums.

They were published at various times during the war and comparison between them can show how certain units were reduced in strength or combined with others to obtain more effective use of the available manpower. They provide the family historian with a picture of the size and make-up of the ancestor's unit and might give a clue to the type of unit.

For example, if a photo shows the ancestor with a group of 12 men standing in front of a repair workshop, it is comforting to note that the war establishment of an ASC Workshop was 12 men and one officer.

If you know that an ancestor had a particular job, e.g. an ambulance driver, then a search through the war establishments would help locate all types of unit that employed ambulance drivers. War establishments will also indicate if men of another corps were attached to the unit.

# 11. MOBILISATION STORES TABLES

These are of very little value to the family historian but give an interesting side light on the ancestor's unit. They consist of a list of every piece of equipment required by a unit down to the smallest detail. For example, the list for an 800 patient casualty clearing station - a tented hospital - includes

122  Tents or Marquees of 5 types
208  Bedsteads
848  Stretchers
 32  Pots, chamber, enamelled
 16  Pots, mustard, enamelled
  1  Whisk, egg

Plus about 200 more items which made up 40 three-ton lorry loads. The location of a full set of these is not known, but they may be found in regimental museums and perhaps among GHQ papers at Kew. The Imperial War Museum (IWM) has about 50 of the forms in Box G of the Army Forms Collection. The Royal Corps of Transport Museum has a similar number but only for ASC units.

# 12. UNIT EMBLEMS

Most divisions of the British Army in France had an emblem which was used to identify lorries and other large items of equipment. Many self-contained corps units had similar signs. At some stage of the war it is believed that orders were given to paint out these emblems as they could be of use to the enemy.

They can help the researcher in several ways. If they appear in any photographs, they can help to identify the unit. Conversely, if the emblem of the ancestor's unit or its associated division can be found, it can be used to identify the unit in the photographs in the IWM.

Emblems usually take the form of a simple 'heraldic' device or an outline that could be painted with the aid of a stencil. Many are illustrated in *British Battle Insignia 1 1914-18 (see* Bibliography Ref. 62). A complete listing is given in *'Divisional and Other Signs'* by Capt. V. Wheeler-Hoolan 1920. This included Australian, Canadian and New Zealand Divisions and gives a history of each and records the reasons for the adoption of their signs. Other sources are the regimental museum, unit histories or photographs of known units.

There is a Military Heraldry Society which takes an interest in such matters. Their magazine, *The Formation Sign*, is available in the Imperial War Museum Printed Books Library. This could be used to locate an expert on WWI emblems. The Photographic Library has several photographs showing sheets of emblems. One of the longest lists of emblems is the 150-card, two-part, series of cigarette cards given away with Players Cigarettes in the 1920s, a selection of these is illustrated in Ref.64. WO161/13 at TNA, Kew contains a short list of some ASC emblems.

To quote an example, a search was being made for a picture of the ancestor's unit, No. 24 Motor Ambulance Convoy, in the Photographic Library. The war diary gives a small sketch of the emblem and describes it as an owl in a ring which the list at TNA quoted above says was a visual pun on the name of the first CO, Capt. Howlett. The library has only a few photos of MACs but one shows 'No. 24 MAC on the St.Pol -Arras Road Feb. 1916'; a second copy in another book says 'No. 27 MAC'. An obvious mistype from a badly written '4' which is proved by the fact that all the cars have a white owl painted within a ring on the side, and that the HQ of No. 24 at that date was half a mile from the St.Pol -Arras Road. No. 27 was stationed many miles away.

# 13. RECRUITING

Did the ancestor volunteer or was he conscripted?

Up to July 1915, the Army consisted of 'Regulars', 'Territorials' and fresh volunteers. These latter formed the basis of the so-called 'New Armies'. By the middle of 1915 it became clear that the war was going to need a lot of men and that the supply of volunteers was not high enough to keep the planned armies at full strength.

The National Registration Act of July 1915 compelled everyone between 15 and 65 to register. By this means the government had at its disposal, by September, a breakdown of the population by sex, age and occupation. This showed that a large number of eligible men not engaged in 'starred' occupations (i.e. not engaged in vital war work) were still available. On the 16th October Lord Derby introduced his so-called *Derby Scheme* which allowed men one last chance to enlist voluntarily.

Those who chose not to volunteer at once could attest with the obligation to come forward if called upon. The attested men were then divided into married and single and split into 23 age 'Groups' between 18 and 41. Some 215,000 volunteered for immediate service and a further 2,910,000 attested. The *Derby Scheme* closed on 15th December 1915. A balance of the figures showed over half a million men still evading service, having neither volunteered nor attested. Conscription was, therefore, introduced on 7 January 1916 for all male British subjects aged between 18 (on 5th August 1915) and 41 (on 2nd March 1916) who were unmarried or widowers without a dependent, on 2nd November 1915. Those called up had no choice of unit.

There were, of course, exemptions for those unfit and those in the indispensable 'starred' trades. The act was extended to married men on 25th May 1916. Those conscripted were divided into age 'Classes' (as opposed to 'Groups' used for *Derby* men) between 18 and 41. Single men in Classes 1 - 23 and married men in Classes 24 - 46 were born between 1875 and 1897.

The actual call up dates were as follows.

*Derby* single men Groups 2 - 5 (aged 19-22) - 25th January 1916 and then in succession up to Group 23 and finally Group 1 on 28th March 1916, at roughly two groups per week. All conscripted single men were called by class beginning on 3rd March and finishing on the 25th March. *Derby* married men were called between 7th March and 13th June 1916 and finally all conscripted men between 3rd and 24th June 1916. Due to a number of exemptions, unfitness, etc., compulsion added only a further 43,000 recruits. In general those under 19 (it was changed to 18 after 3 months training in March 1918,) were not allowed to serve overseas, although there were many who gave false ages. The Army Council Instruction (ACI) which applied from 1st June 1916 defined five classes of fitness - A, B, C, D and E, the first four being subdivided into three sub-classes, e.g. Class A was 'able to march, see to shoot, hear well and stand active service conditions'. Class B2 was 'able to walk five miles to and from work, see and hear sufficiently for ordinary purposes'. The National Archives at Kew has attestation papers in WO96 which for a few regiments extend up to September 1915.

To sum up, if the ancestor was in the Army before September 1915 he was either a regular, reservist or a volunteer, be he part-time Territorial called up for full time service or one who answered Kitchener's call. During the period September 1915 to 13th June 1916 it was still possible to have been a volunteer as the pressures to do so were very high. After 2nd March 1916, for single men, and 25th May, for married men, it was not possible to volunteer, although those who had volunteered before those dates could have had their call-up delayed to as late as 13th June. At about this time the Territorial Force was amalgamated with the Regular Army. (*See* page 150, Vol V, 1916 and page 50, Vol III, 1915 of *the Official History* for further details.) Men usually had to report for duty one month after their group or class was called. The book, *Kitchener's Army*, by Peter Simkins of the Imperial War Museum, deals with recruiting (*see* Bibliography Ref. 61).

The time spent in England during training varied but could be as short as a few months. Leave was granted every four or five months plus a period of two or three days before embarkation. The unit then usually left the country two or three days after return from leave.

In the early days of the war, those who enlisted in their local Territorial Force regiment had certain advantages. Although full time, the soldier in a Territorial regiment was more likely to be at a depot near to his home, and evening passes or even sleeping-out passes were available. Volunteers were also more likely to be able to select the regiment of their own choice rather than being posted by the recruiting officer to a regiment most in need of men. Men in Territorial battalions had to specifically volunteer for overseas service so the new recruit could decide to serve at home, although much pressure would be used to encourage him to sign on for overseas service. In general, Territorial Force Battalions were better equipped and uniformed than the 'Kitchener Battalions'. These advantages disappeared after the first few months of the war.

It appears that each regiment or corps had its own sequence of regimental numbers that it issued to soldiers. There was no universal method or sequence used throughout the army. This meant that if a man changed his regiment he changed his number. It is worth studying lists of numbers for one regiment and trying to obtain a connection between number and date of joining. A good starting point would be the volume of *Soldiers Died in the Great War* covering the ancestor's regiment and the *National Roll of Honour* for the regiment's 'home town' or area. By comparing the two sources, one could probably estimate the ancestor's date of joining from his number. With the ASC, at least, the prefix letters to the number give a clue to the trade and hence to the type of unit. For example, M1 and M2 were mechanics or fitters, DM was driver/mechanic. Each type of trade had its own series of numbers. A glance through *Soldiers Died in the Great War* will trace many more prefixes but will not help to identify them.

# 14. PLACE NAMES AND MAPS

When tracing the ancestor's journeys across France and Belgium, care must be taken not to mistake the places named in various documents. Many of the smaller French villages have similar if not identical names, some only a few miles distant from each other. Some have a second part of the name that differentiates them from their neighbours. This second part is often dropped from entries in war diaries either from lack of knowledge of its significance or just to save time and space. Often the correct name is given in the initial entry but subsequent entries are only in the shortened form. To quote an example, the village of Aubigny can be found some 10 miles NW of Arras and a second one 10 miles east of Amiens, some 30 miles to the south. The former has an added name of Aubigny-en-Artois but the war diary of a unit stationed there only gives the full name once. In this case, both villages were near the Front Line. All this helps to confuse the researcher and care should be taken in checking the location on a map.

Sheet 236 of the Michelin 1/200,000 series covers the whole battle area except, perhaps, the latter days of the war near to the German frontier. Michelin 1/200,000 maps (yellow and blue covers) are available from most good booksellers. Stanfords of Long Acre, London also stock, or will order, the even more detailed and very expensive IGN series, both in the 1/50,000 and 1/25,000 scales (1¼ inches per mile and 2½ inches per mile). Copies of Michelin 1/200,000 sheets 51, 52, 54 (these are sub-sheets of sheet 236), albeit of an old edition, are available with an overprint showing all cemeteries. They can be obtained for a modest cost from the Commonwealth War Graves Commission, 2 Marlow Road, Maidenhead, Berks. SC6 7DX

Even better are the very detailed maps and plans given in the *Official History* as these are to a very large scale and mention the farms and villages used in the diaries. They also use English names given to places and locations by the soldiers that will not be found on modern maps, however detailed. The official maps are also useful in that they have in most cases an overprint showing the armies, army corps and divisions that held a particular part of the Front Line at a specified date. Unfortunately the maps in the *Official History* do not cover areas behind the line to any great extent. Locations of hospitals and other RAMC units can be found on maps in the *History of Medical Services* (*see* Bibliography Ref.26) and transport depots can be found in Ref.21.

Further maps of the battle area in France, and in other war zones, can be found at the TNA, Kew, Class WO153 and WO297 (*see* TNA Record Information Leaflet 115). These maps were originally included with the war diaries and other records, but were extracted and indexed separately.

Many are overlaid with detailed battle dispositions of troops. These often mark the location of individual units or the areas where named reserve units were billeted. This latter point is useful as the *Official History* frequently fails to mention them. (see example maps overleaf)

The index to the maps is arranged in order of the army, army corps and division from whose records they were extracted, and then by date. (The sequence of numbers is often broken up by other non-related entries. Hence, search all the index to check that you have seen all relevant entries.) Therefore, without knowing the area covered by the army, army corps or division at the given date, the desired map may be difficult to locate. Other maps can be found within the war diaries of the staff officers of army corps and armies as these appear to have missed the extraction procedure. Some are also included in the HQ Papers of divisions, army corps and armies in WO158. This latter class is very patchy, some units being well covered and others having no records at all.

Within war diaries, place names were frequently given map references. These are in the form *Sheet 62D E17a*. These refer to a series of maps to a scale of approx. 1/20,000 or 5cm to 1 kilometre (3 inches/mile). The entire battle area was divided into large rectangles each allocated a capital letter (the 'E' in *E17a* ); this rectangle was divided into approximately 30 squares each representing an area of about 1,000 yards by 1,000 yards (some lettered rectangles were divided into 36 squares). Each square was given a number, shown in the centre of the rectangle (the '17'). The 1,000 yard squares are again divided into four 500 yard squares by 2 dotted lines and designated a, b, c, d. The exact point within the 500 yard square was sometimes defined by adding a compass point or position as *E17a central* or *E17aNW*. At this scale the battle covered a large map area so for convenience the grid is divided into numbered sheets. TNA Map Room at Kew does not hold a complete set of these maps but the sheet required may be found within the collections in WO153 mentioned above, although the sheet numbers do not appear in the index. Maps ordered on the computer in the normal way.

An example of the grid system used on Army maps is given below. Samples can be found in a variety of scales. The numbered squares are 1,000 yds square.

The reference for the bridge over the railway can be expressed in several ways of increasing accuracy, viz. Sheet 57c R8d; 57c R8dSE; 57c R8d 6.4 or 57c R8d 65.45. The last method locates the point to within 25 yards.

A section of Sheet 57c showing part of the large square R.

Small square 6 indicates the position of the four lettered sub-divisions. The small letters a, b, c and d do not appear on the map.

The method used to sub-divide the smallest squares. The example reads: 4d 65.45.
The graduations do not appear on the map.

40

During the last few years a collection of large scale maps, known as Trench Maps, have been released. They are held in TNA at Kew under WO 297. They are now also available for purchase on CD Rom.

As an example of the use of detailed maps, consider the photograph in the Imperial War Museum (not reproduced) which shows 'an Advanced Dressing Station on the Montouban-Guillemont Road in September 1916 and also shows two lorries of the 16th (Irish) Division with Shamrocks on the side'. Volume IV of the *Official History* which covers the fighting on the Somme in great detail has a map of a scale of about four or five inches to the mile, which shows the road connecting the two villages. One part of this road is shown tree lined. The stumps of the trees can be seen lining the section of road visible in the photo. Reading the text one can find that 16 Division joined the fighting on the 3rd September and left the front on the 9th September. It would not be until the battle had passed over the village on the 5th or 6th that an ADS would be at that position. Hence one can tie the place and date down very closely. In fact the modern Michelin maps show a war cemetery on the exact spot. It's a sad fact that many men died when help was at hand. A closer look at the photo shows at least one grave already marked in the mud. The *Official History* records show that 16 Division lost over 4,000 men during those few days, over 20% of whom would have been killed.

The knowledge of the map reference is of greater importance than is at first obvious as it is used to find aerial photographs in the Imperial War Museum Photograph Library. They have a very large collection showing areas of ground up to 1 mile square but often much smaller. The negatives are filed by year; sheet no., reference and date taken. Using this index, it is possible to find a bird's eye view of the ancestor's camp taken during the time that he was there.

# 15. LOCATION OF SOURCES

Having outlined the contents of documents such as monthly returns, orders of battle, allocation lists and war diaries, the problem is where to find them. TNA at Kew has most of the information but it is sometimes difficult to locate. As explained, the index to WO 95 (war diaries) is in the form of an order of battle, but unless you know the army, army corps or division with which the ancestor's unit was associated, it means searching through two volumes of the index. Regiments and artillery are easier to find as they are listed by regiment, battalion and brigade at the beginning of the first volume.

It is well worthwhile checking WO95/5467-70 and WO95/5494. The former contains orders of battle for various periods throughout the war and these often have a partial index to units. The latter is a collection of lists, some manuscript and heavily annotated, which give details of unit allocation, changes of unit allocation, locations and postings indexed by location and unit. For some corps there is an index of war diaries arranged in unit number order.

The Imperial War Museum has separate libraries for printed books, manuscripts, photographs and pictures. Entrance can be obtained by telephoned appointment - you must give three or four days' notice. The Printed Book Library will have a selection of books awaiting you if you explain your requirements even in general terms, e.g. 'any histories dealing with the Bedfordshire Regiment'. They hold copies of Becke and GHQ Staff Order of Battle for two dates. They also hold most of the published unit histories as well as copies of regimental journals and magazines.

The Photographic Library has over 5,000,000 pictures for both world wars of which 100,000 date from WWI. Besides being card indexed for town, unit number or name, type of unit, man's name (really only applies to senior officers!) and type of subject, they have hundreds of albums lining the wall where the indexed photos can be viewed. Another section of the albums has the same set of pictures filed according to subject matter. This is well cross-indexed. It's a long shot but you might find a picture of the ancestor's unit showing the ancestor. The collection is still being added to at the rate of 50,000 per year (not all from WWI) but the recent additions are not as well indexed due to staff shortages. This is unfortunate as many photos from old soldiers are now coming to light. Experience has shown that the captions are sometimes inaccurate or incomplete so try to check the photo against a map or unit war diary to ensure you have made the correct selection. Copies of photos can be obtained at a modest price.

The Manuscript Library has many private diaries indexed by unit and unit type. Others can be located with the aid of *Two World Wars - a Guide to Manuscript Collections in the UK. (see* Bibliography Ref.3). A copy is a available on the reference shelves at TNA Kew.

Most regiments and corps have a regimental museum and library. Some, like the Royal Artillery, also have a Historical Society. The quality of the material in libraries varies but it usually includes a set of printed unit histories of the regiment and often much manuscript data. Unfortunately, the curator is often doing it as a part-time job and may not know the value of the records to family history researchers. If you can get inside the record room, you may strike lucky. Some regiments still have lists of pre-war regular soldiers who served throughout the war. They also kept many old photos of groups of men taken at sports events and passing out parades. *A Guide to Military Museums (see* Bibliography Ref. 13) will enable you to locate the museum associated with the ancestor's unit.

Your local library can usually get any of the books so far mentioned through the inter-library loan service but it can take several weeks. The reference shelves often have the standard series of local regimental histories.

The Guildhall Library also has a collection of *Lloyd's Registers of Shipping* which can be a help in identifying the ship used by the ancestor for the trip across the Channel or, for that matter, to any other war zone. The name of the ship is often given in the war diary; if not, check the diaries of those units who went overseas on the same day and who record the same ports of departure and arrival and similar times in their diaries. It often happens that one of these latter documents will list the ship or give other information. Details of the ships are to be found in one of the numerous books on early steam ships (Refs. 51-57). They were usually cross-channel or other ferryboats taken over for the duration of the war by the Admiralty. Canadian cattle boats were often used for horses and other transport.

# 16. BOOKS

Many books have been written about the Great War but only some are of use to the family historian. The 'official' regimental or corps histories often go into great detail and individual companies or units may be mentioned. When dealing with corps this is probably the only place you will find any reference to the ancestor's unit. The corps or regimental journal or magazine often gives an article on a certain type of unit. This is well worth searching for if the type of unit is unusual, as it will probably be the only description available.

For a non-political detailed history of the war, which deals in facts and figures, the *Official History of the War* in 14 volumes is excellent, but difficult to obtain as very few libraries seem to have it and it has a complicated numbering system. With it, one can trace the path of individual battalions or, in some cases, even companies. Chapters IV to VI (1st Jan to 1st July 1916) give a very good description of all the types of unit within the army. In all cases the text concentrates on the main battles and on units in the Front Line. During the time a unit was resting, no mention is made of it, not even the fact that it was resting.

The activities of other corps can be checked in the remaining books of the series as listed in Government Publications Sectional List No. 60.

Many of the more well-known histories deal with politics and strategy and the family historian will find little of interest. The three bibliographies listed in the Bibliography (Nos. 1-3) list numerous books written by soldiers and provide plenty of background information on life in the trenches.

Some of the unit histories listed in Enser and in White (Nos. 1 and 2) may be difficult to find. However, they are very worthwhile trying to locate, even if it means a visit to the Imperial War Museum Library, as they often give a complete roll of the men who served in the unit. This will probably be the only confirmation available. The bibliography which follows (pp. 56-65) is by no means complete but it lists a few books which should be of use to the family historian. Standard bibliographies such as White or Enser run to several hundred pages each.

Once you have discovered the ancestor's unit, check the various units that served with it. In this way you will build up a complete picture of all corps units and battalions who fought with him. Using this list, look up each of the separate units by name and number in the various bibliographies and indexes. In this way you might find a book written on, for example, the field ambulance attached to the ancestor's battalion.

Don't forget the local newspaper. These usually published the list of wounded local men as well as the occasional news item on men serving overseas. Deaths usually rated a picture and a short report, often with extracts from the CO's letter to the next-of-kin. Men given awards for bravery or mentioned in despatches also got a paragraph with, in most cases, a photograph. These, too, often give details of the circumstances of the award, facts that are not available elsewhere. Finding the item can be time-consuming but rewarding. Official advertisements and reports gave lists of men who had failed to answer to their call-up papers and proceedings of the tribunals set up to consider exemption from call-up. These latter sometimes did not give names but in a small village the men can often be identified by the other details published.

Members of the Society of Friends (the Quakers) mostly refused to be called up or served in non-military posts such as the Friends Ambulance Unit. The library at Friends House, Euston Road, London has returns from many of its 'Monthly Meetings', which very roughly equate to Church of England Dioceses. There are about 60-70 returns listing Friends who were called up with details of how and where they served, if at all. There is no index. The library also holds the published history of the Friends Ambulance Unit, which lists names, as well as several books on conscientious objectors.

# 17. USING PHOTOGRAPHS

Many families will still have in their possession photographs of the ancestor in uniform and perhaps others showing a group of men, including the ancestor. These can be of great use to the researcher. Besides the obvious method of identification of the corps or regiment from badges and other insignia there is a method of proving that the photograph in fact shows what it purports to show.

It will often be the case that, after a long search, the ancestor's unit will be deduced from the known facts. A unit will be found that meets all the requirements of date and location but nowhere can a list of names be found that will offer conclusive proof that the ancestor served with that unit. By looking carefully at the picture, *see* if there are any officers, senior NCOs or medal ribbon wearers visible. Can the picture be dated even roughly by service and/or good conduct stripes? The next step is to read the war diary of the unit selected as being that of the ancestor, and which hopefully is the one depicted in the group photograph. Make a list of the names of all officers, NCOs and medal recipients mentioned in the diary. From this it should be possible to put names to at least some of those shown in the photo, taking into account the likely date on which it was taken. Now select the man with the most unusual name and try to find him in the index of births at the Family Records Centre. With holders of gallantry medals, a check should be first made for the *London Gazette* entry as this will give the home town and thus aid the location of the correct reference. If the name is rare the family can usually be located by a few telephone calls to the entries in the phone directory covering the places of birth found from the Family Records Centre or the *London Gazette*.

Should the name be more common, a search should be made to find the marriage at the Family Records Centre (FRC) and, as the indexes give the wife's maiden name after the end of 1911 and also the index to births gives the mother's maiden name from September 1911, the children of that marriage can be located. If the full names of any male children are noted, it should be comparatively easy to contact them as they may still be alive. Armed with a list of possible men, marriages and male children, pay a visit to the FRC or Guildhall Library and search back. Telephone directories, town directories and the *London Gazette* are all at the Guildhall Library, and the library is open on Saturdays.

Having located your contact, first confirm that he is a descendant of the right man, i.e. his father did serve in that unit, did win that medal or has the right army number. Then send him a copy of your photograph. With luck, he will spot his ancestor standing next to yours in the same picture. This proves that, at the time the photograph was taken, both men were together, most likely in the same unit, and as you know the unit of one of the men because his name is in the war diary, the other man, your ancestor, must also have been in the same unit.

It will be noted that the man contacted does not have to know his ancestor's unit. He only has to identify him in a photo and most people can do this even if the soldier was only 20 years old at the time the picture was taken. In case of non-identification, repeat the process with another name. Failure to obtain an identification does not mean you have the wrong unit, only that the man you have selected from the war diary was not there when the picture was taken.

# 18. ARMY LIFE IN FRANCE

To obtain an insight into the life of a soldier in the Great War it is best to read several of the many published soldiers' diaries or compilations of war experiences. However, the family historian might be interested in the following points.

Before 1st March 1916, when volunteering was stopped, a man could join the regiment of his choice, if they would accept him. He could thus travel to the recruiting centre of the regiment, usually in a town in the area bearing the regiment's name, and enlist. If he preferred, he could enlist with his father's 'old regiment' or one associated with his own home town. Alternatively, he could choose one of the corps, e.g. ASC or RE, especially if he had a trade, as they often paid more. The ordinary soldier was paid one shilling a day while certain skilled men could earn six shillings a day. After 1916 men enlisted anywhere and were posted according to their skills and the requirements of the army.

Once enlisted, training began and normally took several months although at times of great need the period was shortened. No leave would be granted for a period of at least 10-15 weeks although an evening pass to visit a nearby town could be obtained. After that, men were released in turn to go on leave every 20 weeks or so. In most cases this meant no leave before the time came to sail for France. It was then usual to grant 48 or 72 hours leave to the whole unit. Upon return from leave, four days were spent packing, etc. and by the fifth day the unit was on the way to the port. If a complete division was assembled in England, *Becke* says it was customary for the King to inspect it before sailing.

A man could go to France as part of a complete unit, i.e. a battalion or ASC Company, or as part of a draft, which was a group of men who would be allocated to another unit or units once in France. On the other side of the Channel a short stay would be made at a large transit camp. Here the completed units could wait until all the men and vehicles had crossed before proceeding further. The drafts would wait until their final destination was determined, then they would be given the appropriate cap badges and sent up to the line to join their unit. It can be seen that your ancestor might already have changed regiment or, more commonly, his battalion.

Transport to the Front Line would be by train and finally by marching. Mechanised units could use their own vehicles. Up to 1916, when Nissen huts began to be introduced, men stationed behind the line such as transport, medical and supply units would live in barns or tents. Officers would be billeted in a house. Beds or bunks were unknown, the men sleeping on the ground or on straw. Within a short time everyone was covered with lice and fleas which could not be got rid of until the return to England.

When men were stationed nearer the front, shell fire forced the men into dugouts in the ground or into cellars of ruined houses. Gun crews were often subject to enemy counter-battery fire and hence they also lived in dugouts. In certain areas movement on the roads, if any were left, brought an immediate hail of shells. Hence, all work tended to be done at night.

For the fighting men in the Front Line, the situation was much worse. Each unit would spend a period in the first line trench. This entailed leaving most of their kit behind at the transport area perhaps two or three miles behind the front. Then, encumbered with extra ammunition, hand grenades, entrenching tools and other items for survival, often weighing 60-70 pounds, they would march forward at night to take over the trench within 50-300 yards of the German lines. The last mile or more of the approach might itself be along a communication trench, knee deep in water. Once in the Front Line trench they would have to stay there day and night till relieved in 4-15 days. At times they had to 'stand-to', i.e. stand up on a raised 'shelf' (the firing step) in the trench ready to shoot over no-man's-land. At other times they could 'stand down' or in other words stay at the bottom of the trench often deep in mud. To sleep they took it in turns to crawl into narrow recesses scooped out of the sides of the trench. When relieved they retired to a second line perhaps 100-200 yards to the rear where living conditions were a little better. Here they were often called upon at night to come forward, past the Front Line, into no-man's-land to put up barbed wire defences or to help rebuild trenches damaged by shell fire. Food for both lines would be brought up by fatigue parties from the cooks stationed near the transport. This often took two to three hours due to the mud and shell fire.

Their turn of duty in the trenches finished, the unit would retire to the rear area and try to relax although they still had to sleep in dugouts and cellars as they were within shelling range. Nights were spent moving supplies to the Front Line from rearward depots or providing working parties to repair or make roads and railways. After a week or 10 days the cycle would repeat itself. With luck they might have been able to visit a bath house during this time where they could have a hot bath or shower and a change of underwear; however, the fleas always survived the cleaning.

After one or two months the whole unit would withdraw several miles, usually beyond shelling range. Here they could rest, train and help with transport and repairs. With luck they could live in barns, etc. above ground and move freely at all times. The whole cycle would repeat itself again after about a month.

At less frequent intervals, the division and then the corps would be withdrawn into reserve so that all units contained within them could enjoy a period well away from the front. The time was spent in training or rehearsing new attacks.

Most of the time in the Front Line trench was spent watching; occasionally a small raid would be made on the enemy to capture a prisoner. The total length of the famous named battles took only about one third of all the time between 1914 and 1918. Hence, on any one stretch of front, battles were comparatively rare. Some parts were inactive right up to the last three months of the war. However, units were switched from one part to another so that 'fresh' troops could be used in a heavy attack. Units of fighting troops involved in an attack could lose 50% of their strength in killed and wounded. In some cases it was even more. The numbers would be made up with fresh drafts of men from England. No records of the names of these latter still exist.

The men of the various corps represented about one third to one half of the total army strength and those units allocated as divisional troops had a more dangerous time than corps, army or lines of communication troops.

Divisional artillery was often under shell fire from the opposing side; Royal Engineers Signal sections would frequently have to lay or repair telephone cables in sight of the enemy and companies of Royal Engineers would work in no-man's-land laying barbed wire. However, during their non-working periods they could retire to the comparative safety of a dug-out or billet in a cellar a mile or two behind the line.

Life would continue like this seven days a week, 52 weeks a year until home leave was granted. The length of leave was increased from 10 to 14 days (both times including travel) on 1st November 1917. In December 1917 over 115,000 men in France had had no leave for over 12 months and some 5,000 none for 18 months. By January 1918, 5,500 officers and men were being sent on leave each day, itself quite a transport problem. Journey time from Front Line trench to front door was under 48 hours for most places in England and Wales. For officers at least, they could choose to take their leave in the south of France.

At the end of the war, men were demobilised from about December 1918 onwards. Men in important industries, like miners, were released first; followed in order by others of lower priority. Most men were home by May or June 1919 except those forming the Army of the Rhine or those fighting in Russia.

# 19. RESEARCH METHODS

These depend to a large extent on what the researcher aims to achieve, but the research can usually be split into several phases. First the tracing of the exact unit in which the ancestor served; then the obtaining of background information on the history of that unit in relation to a general knowledge of what took place during the war. Finally, an attempt could be made to find evidence of the ancestor's service. Perhaps a photograph could be found in the archives or a mention of his name in one of the few extant documents.

The most difficult step is the first - that is to find the unit. Those who have family evidence giving precise details will have saved themselves a great deal of trouble. For those not in this fortunate position, the procedure is as follows.

First of all, make out a list of all the known facts and unsubstantiated data on the ancestor's career (Fig.1 shows a typical list). Try to put everything down in writing before any deductions are made or research is done. This will prevent the twisting of the truth in order to make the ancestor's history fit the research findings - a trap into which it is very easy to fall and which can completely mislead the researcher. The aim is to find a unit that matches the list in every respect.

With 'regimental' ancestors use the two bibliographies given in the reference section to find a detailed history of the regiment during the war. In most cases this will provide enough facts to tie the unit down to one battalion. Failing this a search will have to be made using Becke or one or more volumes of the *Official History*. Problems arise if no one battalion matches all the data on the list. This often indicates a transfer to another unit. Becke may give a hint in this respect as he gives dates of mergers and disbandments.

Other warning signs of a change of unit are the presence of the ancestor back in England after a period abroad or knowledge of his being wounded. It was common practice for men returning to France after wounding to be posted to the Labour Corps. Also, does the date of leaving England (if known) correspond to the departure date of the battalion. If not it could mean a transfer to another battalion while waiting in the base camp in France.

Once the battalion has been identified, it is well worth making a list of every village and town at which it was stationed; also a list of each division, corps or army in which it served. These lists should include dates. The information can be obtained from books and war diaries. Using these lists, check each item in the indexes in the Imperial War Museum Photograph Library. It is possible, though not likely, that the ancestor appears on a photograph. The Imperial War Museum has over 100,000 photos of WWI - if each shows only 10 men, that is one million or a fifth of all the men who served in France. A one in five chance is well worth a search. The same lists of locations can be used to find diaries in the Imperial War Museum Library or books from the bibliography. In this way it is possible to check small details of the ancestor's story.

Approximately 32 motor ambulance convoys served in France. The Imperial War Museum Photograph Library has pictures of four of these. No. 22 is shown in a series of 10 pictures, a large number of officers and men are visible. Some men are also to be seen in a picture of a second unit.

With corps or Royal Artillery ancestors, the task is usually more difficult. Not only is the family data less likely to give the unit identification but the number of units is far higher. The best chance of success lies with having enough data to identify the type of unit. Even chance remarks such as, 'He always said that he caught his rheumatism lying on his back on the wet ground repairing lorries', will go a long way towards finding the unit. Once again this should be on the data sheet before a serious start is made on your research.

By studying corps histories some idea of the variety and types of units should be obtained. The next step would be to compile lists of all suitable units of the corps that were in the same area as the ancestor at the correct dates. These can be drawn up by reference to the monthly returns (for first date in France), GHQ orders of battle and war diaries.

It is best to include all units that served with the army covering the ancestor's location at that time. The army boundaries can be found in general histories and corps histories but they changed frequently and due account of this fact should be taken when compiling the list. In addition, those lines of communication and GHQ troops serving in an army area should be included. If the order of battle does not give this information, then they should all be included until they can be eliminated by reference to the individual war diaries which, of course, give the precise location at any date. The list can contain 50 or 70 units but if further lists can be drawn up for two or more dates and corresponding locations of the ancestor, the researcher will find that only a few units appear in all lists. This brings the number down to a manageable size and the war diaries of these few can be studied to *see* if any clues can be found to make a more positive identification of the ancestor's unit. (*See* Fig 2.)

Despite a possible unit having been identified, proof may be very difficult, as very few lists of men remain. As with regiments, a complete list of dates and locations of the unit should be made and these checked in the indexes of the Imperial War Museum. The chances of finding books or diaries by a member of the unit are probably smaller than with a soldier serving in a battalion as the number of men per unit is somewhat less than the battalions's 1000. However, the proportion of names being mentioned in the war diary is somewhat higher as the officer-in-charge would know each man by name.

The war diaries of units which served alongside the ancestor's should always be examined as they can give extra information.

As an example, the ancestor's unit was stated in the war diary to have arrived at Rouen at 5 pm on 18th March 1916 but the name of the ship is not mentioned. While drawing up the list of units which sailed for France within the defined period, it was noticed that two similar units sailed on the same day. The war diaries of these two units were checked and one recorded that the unit also arrived at Rouen at 5 pm on 18th March 1916 and gave the name of the ship. In addition all three diaries reported that the date for leaving the Base Depot in London was postponed for four days but only one reported the fact that four inches of snow fell overnight before the original departure date, thus making the task of driving 50 ambulances to Avonmouth almost impossible.

Some units contained men from two corps, for example a heavy artillery battery would be made up of the gun crews from the Royal Artillery and transport drivers and mechanics from the Army Service Corps. In these cases, it is wise to check records in both corps museums. War establishments (q.v., page 24) will give details of this double manning.

The ancestor served with a motor ambulance convoy which was an RAMC unit although most of the men were from the ASC. The RAMC Museum had very few records on MACs of any description but the ASC Museum was able to produce a three-page history of the ancestor's unit written by the second in command, an ASC Captain.

A great deal of effort was expended in making camp sites and dugouts as comfortable as possible, hence when a unit was posted elsewhere, the unit taking over its duties usually took over its camp site and other facilities. Sometimes the unit's war diary mentions the previous occupant of the site but in any case it is worth checking which unit preceded or succeeded the ancestor's unit and searching its war diary as well as this will add details of the site conditions.

# 20. BIBLIOGRAPHY

Dewey Index Numbers for World War 1 are:

### General History

| | |
|---|---|
| 940.4144 | General Description of Fighting |
| 940.42B | Battles |
| 940.465 | War Graves |
| 940.48141 | War diaries of Soldiers |
| 355.00941 | Military Museums |
| 355.10 | Daily Life of Soldiers |
| 355.134 | Badges |
| 355.14 } 355.31 } | Uniform |
| 356.11 | Unit Histories |

### Companion Volumes to this publication (all published by the Federation of Family History Societies):

1. *The Location of British Army Records 1914-1918*
2. *More Sources of World War I Army Ancestry*
3. *Identifying Your World War I Soldier from Badges and Photographs*

### General Publications

1. *A Subject Bibliography of the First World War*. A.G.S. Enser. (Andre Deutsch.) Lists books by subject, town name, battle name, unit name and unit type.
2. *A Bibliography of Regimental Histories*. A.S. White. Deals with all periods, not just WWI. Indexed by Regiment and Corps names. Now also available on CD Rom.
   (Some of the books listed in the above bibliographies may have been published privately by Regiments and units. Copies may only exist in the Imperial War Museum Library or the Regimental Museum).
3. *Two World Wars - a Guide to Manuscript Collections in the UK*. S.L. Mayer and W.J. Koenig. (Bowker, London 1976.) A copy is a available on the reference shelves at TNA Kew.
4. *A Guide to Sources of British Military History*. Robin Higham.

5. *Family History Sources: The Two World Wars*. Clive Vaisey. Vol 2 No 3 July 1981, Journal of NW Kent FHS. Mentions St. Catherine's Indexes (now the Family Records Centre), War Graves Commission and war diaries.
6. *Army Records: Tracing my Grandfather.* Jean Allen. Vol I No 8 October 1980, Journal of NW Kent FHS. Gives an example of records from Army Search, Hayes.
7. The National Archives Leaflet No 59, *British Military Records as Sources of Biography and Genealogy*.
8a. *Tracing your Ancestors in the Public Record Office*. Amanda Bevan and Andrea Duncan. Fourth Edition, London HMSO. ISBN 0 11 440222 1. Section 18.31 deals with records after 1913 and mentions pensions records in PMG 9, PMG 42, PMG 11 and PMG 44 to 47. A few deaths are listed in RG 35/45 to 69.
8b. TNA Leaflet No 40, *Operational Records of the British Army in the Great War 1914-19*.
9. *Finding the Men who Fought in the Trenches*. Norman Holding. *Family Tree Magazine*, Vol 2 No 6 (Sept/Oct 1986) and Vol 3 No 1 (Nov 1986). Two articles dealing with research methods.
10. *History of the First World War*. B.G. Liddell Hart. (Pan Books, 1972.) First published circa 1933. A one-volume general history full of strategy and politics.
11. *Field Marshal Haig's Despatches*. Edited by John Terraine. Published after the War with a commentary. Makes a very readable factual account of the War from December 1915 to 1918. Not too much politics and a fair amount of detail of the battles and units concerned. If you can't get the *Official History* with its 14 volumes, this is a good substitute, but it does not start until December 1915.
12. *A Register of the Regiments and Corps of the British Army*. Arthur Swinson. (Archive Press, London.) This gives a brief history of the units and enables you to identify the modern successor to the WW1 unit.
13. *A Guide to Military Museums*. Compiled by Terence Wise. 10th edn. 2001. (Imperial Press.) This gives the location of Military Museums by their modern names.
14. *Army Service Records of the First World War*. William Spencer. TNA Publications, 2001. Gives full details of both 'Burnt' and 'Unburnt Docs' together with examples.

15. *British Regiments 1914-18*. Brig. E.A. James. (Samson Books, 1978.) This is a reprint in one volume of two earlier books by the same author dealing with Infantry and Cavalry regiments. It can be found on open shelves in the Imperial War Museum and the The National Archives, Kew.

16. *Discovering British Cavalry Regiments.* Arthur Taylor. (Shire Publications Limited.) Only a very slim book, included in this list because it is often sold on Family History Society bookstalls.

17. *Locations of British Cavalry, Infantry and Machine Gun Units 1914-24*. Robert W. Gould MBE.

18. *Famous Regiments.* Edited by Lt.-Gen. Sir Brian Horrocks. (Leo Cooper Ltd., London.) About 50 volumes covering most of the regiments and corps - found in most libraries but they are not usually detailed enough on the Great War period.

19. *Royal Army Service Corps- A History of Transport and Supply in the British Army.* Vol 2. Col. R.H. Beadon. (Cambridge University Press, 1930.) This volume deals with the Great War.

20. A history of various ASC UK depots is given in WO161/30, WO161/12 and 13 and WO95/5466.

21. *Transportation on the Western Front 1914-18.* Col. A.M. Henniker. One volume plus separate box of maps. This deals with railway, road and vehicle transport. Only of value to those having ancestors in the ASC, RE and RAOC.

22. *The Work of the Royal Engineers in the European War 1914-18*. The R.E. Institution 1921-27. Chatham, Kent. Includes volumes on the Signal Service and water.

23. *History of the Corps of Royal Engineers*. Vol 5. Brig.-Gen. W. Baker Brown. Published 1952, 728 pages. Covers the Home Front, France, Flanders and Italy in WWI. Vol 6 covers activities in the Middle East 1914-1919.

24. *History of the Ordnance Services*. Maj.-Gen. A. Forbes. (Medici Society, London, 1929.)

25. *The Great War and the R.A.M.C.* F.S.Brereton. (Constable, London, 1919.) Goes into real detail but only deals with first two or three months of the war. Vol 1 was the only one published.

26. *Medical History of the Great War*. *General History*. Maj.-Gen. Sir W.G. MacPherson in four volumes. Vol 1 Medical Services in UK and African campaigns; Vol 2 Medical Services on the Western Front 1914-15

(includes descriptions of all types of RAMC unit); Vol 3 Medical Services on the Western Front 1916, 1917, 1918 and Italy (includes allocations of RAMC units); Vol 4 Medical Services in Gallipoli, Macedonia, Mesopotamia, North-west Persia, Aden, East Africa and North Russia. Also Ambulance Transport during the War. (A summary of types of vehicles and stretchers.)

27. *Veterinary Services*. Maj.-Gen. Sir L. J. Blenkinsop and Lt.-Col. J.W. Ramsey. One volume. With (29), would be of interest to those investigating men who served with the ASC Ambulance Convoys, RAMC and Veterinary Units.

28. Government Publications Sectional List No 60. HMSO. Includes a long list of books published by HMSO. Most are in the series *History of the Great War Based on Official Documents by Direction of the Historical Section of the Committee of Imperial Defence* (examples given in Nos. 29, 32, 34, 35), often known simply as the *Official History*. Another list of the *Official History* will be found in *Stand To!*, No.20 Summer 1990 (The journal of the Western Front Association).

29. The *Official History* is divided into several groups of volumes of which *Military Operations* forms a part. *France and Belgium* has 14 vols. mainly written by Brig.-Gen. Sir James E. Edmonds. Dates of publication cover the period 1922-1949. In recent years a number of volumes have been re-published, some without the map volume that accompanied the first edition. Further editions of some of the volumes are being published by the Imperial War Museum.

*France and Belgium*. All by Brig.-Gen. Sir James E. Edmonds unless otherwise stated.

1914 Vol 1. *1914 August-October. Mons, the Retreat to the Seine, the Marne and the Aisne*. With a case of maps. Editions 1922, 1925, 1934. The 1934 edition was reprinted by Shearer Publications in 1984.

1914 Vol 2. *1914 October-November. Antwerp, La Bassee, Armentieres, Messines and Ypres*. With a case of maps. 1925.

1915 Vol 1. (with Capt. G. C. Wynne). *Winter 1914-15. Neuve Chapelle-Ypres, December 1914-May 1915*. With a case of maps. 1927.

1915 Vol 2. *Aubers Ridge, Festubert and Loos*. With a case of maps. 1928.

1916 Vol 1 *1916 to July 1. The Somme*. With a case of maps. 1927. Reprinted by Shearer Publications in 1986.

1916 Vol 1 *Appendices Volume*, 1927.

1916 Vol. 2 *1916, July 2 to End of Somme Battle*. With a case of maps and Appendices.

1917 Vol 1 (Capt. Cyril Falls) *The German Retreat to the Hindenburg Line and the Arras Battles*. With a case of Maps and separate volume of Appendices, 1940.

1917 Vol 2 *June 7-November 10. Messines and Third Ypres (Passchendaele).* 1949.

1917 Vol 3 (Capt. W. Mills) *The Battle of Cambrai*. 1949.

1918 Vol 1 *March Offensive*. With a case of maps and separate volume of Appendices. 1935.

1918 Vol 2 *March-April*. With a case of maps. 1937.

1918 Vol 3 *May-July*. 1939.

1918 Vol 4 *August 8-September 28. Franco-British Offensive*. 1947.

1918 Vol 5 *September 28-November 10*. 1947.

There are also volumes for East Africa (1), Egypt and Palestine (2), Gallipoli (2), Italy (1), Macedonia (2), Mesopotamia (4), Togoland and the Cameroons (1) and Persia (1).

The occupation of Germany in 1919 is covered by Brig.-Gen. Sir James E. Edmonds in *The Occupation of the Rhineland 1918-1929*. This was only published in draft form which is in TNA, Kew (CAB 44. or CAB 45). However, this was published by the Imperial War Museum in 1988.

When you know your ancestor's unit and something about its battles, this series is a must - it goes into great detail. Chapters IV to VI of France and Belgium 1916 Vol 1, *1916 to July 1st. The Somme*, gives an overall picture of the make-up of the British Army in 1916 right down to the Army Typewriter Service and the Rubber Stamp Factory. Page 12 in 1915 Vol. 1 has a list of Army Schools.

30. *Order of Battle of British Armies in France*. Gen. Staff GHQ, published many times during the war. There are two issues in the Imperial War Museum Library. Others are in regimental museums. There is a set in TNA Kew (WO95/5467-5470) which is believed to be complete. This book gives a sort of organisational family tree of the army in France. It gives far more detail about allocated units than Becke but does not relate units to battles. Shows the situation at the date of the issue. Enables the tracing of units not given in, i.e. lines of communication, army and corps troops (*see* also Note 6). The issue for 11th November 1918 was published by the Imperial War Museum in February 1989 (ISBN 0 90 1627 49 6).

31. *Order of Battle of Divisions* Compiled by Major A.F. Becke. (London, HMSO, 1945.) In four parts, parts 2 and 3 each requiring two volumes.

Part 1. The Regular British Divisions (1st-9th).

Part 2a. The Territorial Force, Mounted Divisions and 1st Line Territorial Force Divisions (42nd-56th).

Part 2b. The 2nd Line Territorial Force Divisions (57th-69th) plus the Home Service Divisions (71st-73rd ) and the 74th and 75th Divisions.

Part 3a. The New Army Divisions (9th-26th).

Part 3b. The New Army Divisions (30th-41st) and 63rd (RN) Division.

Part 4. The Army Council, GHQ's Armies and Corps, 1914-1918.

These volumes have been reprinted as follows: Part 1 Sherwood Press 1986; Part 2a Sherwood Press 1987; Part 2b Westlake Military Books 1988; Parts 3a and 3b in one volume by Westlake Military Books 1989.

The above books give a brief history of each army, corps or division, together with a list of battles and other actions in which they took part. With the divisions it gives the brigades and battalions allocated to each for four or five intervals throughout the war. Allocation of Royal Artillery Brigades, ASC and other units is also given with many footnotes to explain deviations. [*See* also GHQ Staff Order of Battle (Note 6) which is not the same book nor does it give the same information.] *See* Figs. 6 and 7. This book is a must for family historians wishing to trace their ancestor's war service. The reprinting of this series will make it far more available. The Imperial War Museum Printed Books Library has two sets, one with handwritten corrections. It is unfortunate that there is no index.

32. *Soldiers Died in the Great War 1914-18*. (London, HMSO, 1921). In 80 paperbacked parts plus one for officers. Entries by corps and regiments, subdivided into battalions; names then in alphabetical order. Gives name, number, where born, where enlisted (plus home town if different), when died and war zone. Does not give corps unit but gives previous battalions if transferred. All 80 volumes, plus the companion volume of *Officers Died in the Great War*, have now been reprinted and are obtainable from, among others, the Imperial War Museum at prices of between £10 and £35. ISBN 1871505 01 1 - 1 871505 80 1. The rolls for both officers and soldiers are now available on a single CD Rom.

33. *The National Roll of the Great War 1914-18*. This was published by the National Publishing Co., London. A total of 14 volumes appeared, the

last in 1922. It is believed that the company then went into liquidation before the whole work could be completed. The method of obtaining the information is not known but some men whose names appear cannot recall being approached for details. Also a man who is known to have served in several units is listed as having only one posting. The 14 volumes are difficult to find, but there is a complete set in the Printed Books Library of the Imperial War Museum. Those marked * in the list following are also in the Society of Genealogists' Library.

| | | | |
|---|---|---|---|
| Vol 1 | London* | Vol 8 | Leeds* |
| Vol 2 | London* | Vol 9 | Bradford |
| Vol 3 | London* | Vol 10 | Portsmouth |
| Vol 4 | Southampton | Vol 11 | Manchester |
| Vol 5 | Luton* | Vol 12 | Bedford and Northampton* |
| Vol 6 | Birmingham | Vol 13 | London* |
| Vol 7 | London* | Vol 14 | Salford |

The names are given in alphabetical order with the full home address. In some volumes the listing is divided into two or three parts. Each part must be searched and no hint is given that the volume is divided. Take care! Sometimes gives battalion number; other times only regiment. Maximum number of men mentioned is about 150,000-200,000, i.e. about 1 in 20 or 1 in 30. Some entries have been found to be inaccurate.

34. *The War Graves of the British Empire*. Over 200 volumes, one for each cemetery. Subtitled *The Register of the Names of Those who Fell in the Great War and are Buried in the . . . . . . . . Cemetery*. Compiled and published by order of the Imperial War Graves Commission, London, 1923. A copy of the appropriate volume is to be found in a bronze wall safe at each Cemetery. May be in some reference libraries. The Commonwealth War Graves Commission[1], 2 Marlow Road, Maidenhead, Berks, SL6 7DX may be able to look up a name. Gives the following details: name, number, where born, where enlisted (plus home town if different), when died, next of kin. Gives battalion but not corps unit number. Also gives previous unit if transferred. Now also available on the internet at www.cwgc.com

35. *Soldiers Killed on the First Day of the Somme*. Ernest W. Bell. Lists 18,000 names with rank, regiment and number who died on 1st July 1916.

---

[1] The Imperial War Graves Commission became the Commonwealth War Graves Commission by Charter in 1964.

36. *Badges and Insignia of British Armed Services*. Major W.Y. Carmen and Dr Tanner (Adam and Chas. Black, London).
37. *Awards of Honour*. Capt. Arthur Jocelyn C.V.O. (Adam and Chas. Black, London).
38. *Head Dress Badges of the British Army*. A.L. Kipling and H.L. King (Fred. Muller, London).
39. *For Gallantry in the Performance of Military Duty*. A list of awards of the Meritorious Service Medal (MSM) for gallantry contains rank, number, name, unit, theatre of war and several citations. 64 pages.
40. *The Medals, Decorations and Orders of the Great War 1914-1918*. A.A. Purves. 220 pages. 150 ribbons in full colour.
41. Numerous books by J.M.A. Tamplin dealing with the recipients of various medals. These will assist you to identify units from photos and medals.

During the War several monthly or weekly illustrated magazines were published. These are full of background detail and many pictures. Typical of these are the next three:

42. *The Great War. A Standard History of the All Europe Conflict*. Edited by H.W. Wilson and J.A. Hammerton. (Amalgamated Press, London.) 27 volumes.
43. *The Times History of the Great War*. 20 volumes.
44. *The War Budget*. Published weekly by the Daily Chronicle.
45. *I Was There*. The human story of the Great War 1914-18. Editorial by Sir John Hammerton. (The Waverley Book Co. Ltd., London about 1938-40.) About 360 eyewitness accounts taken from named but undated printed sources. 4 volumes. Many photos, most from Imperial War Museum Photo Library, but unfortunately not numbered.
46. *They Called it Passchendaele*. Lyn Macdonald. (Michael Joseph, London.). A collection of eyewitness accounts recorded in 1979-80 which was used as the basis of a BBC broadcast.
47. *Roses of No-Mans-Land*. Lyn Macdonald. Stories by and about nurses. Also a BBC broadcast and Channel 4 television documentary (1997).
48. *Death's Men - Soldiers of the Great War* Denis Winter. (Allen Lane.) Life in the trenches.
49. *Men of Gallipoli*. Peter Liddle. (Allen Lane, London, 1976.) Has an extensive bibliography and a list of 600 men whose memoirs are available at the Brotherton Library (Leeds University) in the Liddle Archives.

50. *Before Endeavours Fade*. Rose E.B. Coombs. (Battle of Britain Prints International Limited, London, 1976.) A guide to the battlefields as they exist today. Also gives a short history of the Imperial War Graves Commission.

Most Libraries have a selection of 'shipping' books around 387.24. A few of these are:

51. *British Vessels Lost at Sea 1914-18*. A reprint of the official HMSO 1919 edition. (Patrick Stephens, 1977.) ISBN 0850592917. Beware! The page number sequence is in two sections each with a separate index. A large part of the book is taken up by a list of ships which were attacked but not sunk or even hit! Hence it includes a large proportion of troopship and transport fleets.

52. *A Century of Cross Channel Passenger Ferries*. Ambrose Greenaway. (Ian Allen, 1981.)

53. *Paddle Steamers 1837-1914*. Richard Clammer (B.T. Batford.)
    (The previous two items contain extensive bibliographies which should enable the researcher to find details of any ship.)
    The following four may also be of interest.

54. *Cross Channel and Coastal Paddle Steamers.* F. Burtt. (R. Gilling, 1934.)

55. *Irish Passenger Steamship Service*. 2 volumes. D.B. McNeill. (David and Charles, 1972.) Has a list of locations and photographs.

56. *Railway and Other Steamers*. C.L.D. Duckworth. (T. Stephenson and Sons Limited, 1968.)

57. *Hospital Ships and Ambulance Trains.* Lt.-Col. John H. Plumridge. (*See* ley, Service and Co., London, 1975.) This gives a very full history of these two types of RAMC transport.

58. A draft history of ASC units in Mesopotamia is given in WO161/17-19.

59. *Royal Artillery Commemoration Book 1914-18*. Vols 1 and 2. (G. Bell and Son Limited, London.)

60. There are three periodicals which cover the War and a look through back copies will reveal many additional books as well as articles on units and actions.
    (a) *Stand To* the journal of the Western Front Association. Three issues per year since 1980. Numbers 1-30 (Winter 1990).
    (b) *Bulletin* - the 'in-house' general news letter of the Western Front Association. Three issues per year since 1982. Numbers 1 to 49 (April 1997). Both these publications are available to members of the Western Front Association. Subscription £20.00. Membership Sec. 6 Church Stree Kidderminster DY10 2AD. There is also:

(c) *The Great War 1914-18* - the illustrated journal of the First World War History Group. Available from Broadsword Publishing, 6 Cranleigh Gardens, Sanderstead, South Croydon, Surrey CR2 9LD. £15.00 for four issues. About four issues per year. First published 1988.

Copies of these journals are available in the Imperial War Museum Printed Books Library.

61. *Kitchener's Army*. The Raising of the New Armies 1914-16. Peter Simkins. (Manchester University Press, 1990) 0 7190 2638 5. Paperback.

62. *British Battle Insignia. (1) 1914-18*. Mike Chappell. (Osprey Publishing, London, 1995.) ISBN 0 85045 727 0. No. 182 of the Osprey Men-at-Arms Series.

63. Article *The Role and Composition of the Army Corps in the BEF* Page 191 No. 22 Summer 1990 *Stand To* the journal of the Western Front Association.

64. *World War One British Army* (Brassey's History of Uniforms Series) by Stephen Bull (Brasseys, London 1998)

65. *British Tommy 1914-18* Martin Pegler & Mike Chappell (Osprey Warrior Series No.16. 1996)

66. *British Army Territorial Units 1914-18* (Osprey Men at Arms Series No.245) Ray Westlake & Mike Chappell 1991

67. *The British Army 1914-18* (Osprey Men at Arms Series NO. 81 R.J.Marrion & G.A.Embleton 1978

68. *The Old Contemptibles* (Osprey Elite Series No.24) Michael Barthorpe & Pierre Turner 1989

69. *The World War One Source Book by* Philip Heythornwaite. Arms & Armour Press 1994.

# APPENDIX I

A list of the cavalry regiments, infantry regiments and corps of the British Army who served in the Great War 1914-18. The names given are those in use during that period.

## CAVALRY

### Household Cavalry
Life Guards - 1st and 2nd Regiments
Royal Horse Guards
Household Cavalry Composite Regiment. Formed from elements of the above three regiments.
Household Battalion. Formed from elements of the Household Cavalry but they fought as infantry.
Guards Divisional Cavalry Squadron. Formed from 1st Life Guards Reserve Regiment.

### Dragoon Guards
1st (King's) Dragoon Guards
2nd Dragoon Guards (Queen's Bays)
3rd (Prince of Wales's) Dragoon Guards
4th (Royal Irish) Dragoon Guards
5th (Princess Charlotte of Wales's) Dragoon Guards
6th Dragoon Guards (Carabiniers)
7th (Princess Royal's) Dragoon Guards

### *Cavalry of the Line*
1st Royal Dragoons
2nd Dragoons (Scots Greys)
3rd (King's Own) Hussars
4th (Queen's Own) Hussars
5th (Royal Irish) Lancers
6th (Inniskilling) Dragoons
7th (Queen's Own) Hussars
8th (King's Royal Irish) Hussars
9th (Queen's Royal) Lancers

10th (Prince of Wales's) Own Royal Hussars
11th (Prince Albert's Own) Hussars
12th (Prince of Wales's Royal) Lancers
13th Hussars
14th (King's) Hussars
15th (The King's) Hussars
16th (The Queen's) Lancers
17th (Duke of Cambridge's Own) Lancers
18th (Queen Mary's Own) Hussars
19th (Queen Alexandra's Own Royal) Hussars
20th Hussars
21st (Empress of India's Own) Lancers

## Cavalry Reserve
1st King Edward's Horse (The King's Overseas Dominions Regiment)
2nd King Edward's Horse (The King's Overseas Dominions Regiment)

## Dragoons (Reserve)
4th Reserve Regiment Dragoons
Old 1st Reserve Cavalry Regiment (1st and 5th Dragoon Guards)
Old 2nd Reserve Cavalry Regiment (2nd Dragoon Guards and
    6th Dragoons)
Old 3rd Reserve Cavalry Regiment (3rd and 6th Dragoon Guards)
Old 4th Reserve Cavalry Regiment (4th and 7th Dragoon Guards)
Old 5th Reserve Cavalry Regiment (1st and 2nd Dragoons)
6th Reserve Regiment of Dragoons

## Hussars (Reserves)
2nd Reserve Regiment of Cavalry
3rd Reserve Regiment of Cavalry
5th Reserve Regiment of Cavalry

## Lancers (Reserve)
1st Reserve Regiment of Lancers
Old 6th Reserve Cavalry Regiment (5th and 12th Lancers)
Old 7th Reserve Cavalry Regiment (9th and 21st Lancers)
Old 8th Reserve Cavalry Regiment (16th and 17th Lancers)

No 2 Cavalry Depot
No 3 Cavalry Depot
No 5 Cavalry Depot

North Irish Horse
South Irish Horse

## Dragoons (Territorials)
2nd County of London
Shropshire Yeomanry
Queen's Own Yorkshire Dragoons
North Somerset Yeomanry
Duke of Lancaster's Own Yeomanry
Hampshire Yeomanry
Derbyshire Yeomanry
Hertfordshire Yeomanry
Berkshire Yeomanry
Montgomeryshire Yeomanry
Lothian and Border Horse
Queen's Own Royal Glasgow Yeomanry
Fife and Forfar Yeomanry
Norfolk Yeomanry
Sussex Yeomanry
Glamorganshire Yeomanry
Essex Yeomanry
Northamptonshire Yeomanry
Lovat Scouts
Scottish Horse Yeomanry

## Lancers (Territorials)
Lanarkshire Yeomanry
Surrey Yeomanry
Lincolnshire Yeomanry
Bedfordshire Yeomanry
East Riding of Yorkshire Yeomanry
City of London Yeomanry

## Hussars (Territorials)

Ayrshire (Earl of Carrick's Own) Hussars Yeomanry
The Royal Buckinghamshire Hussars
The Denbighshire Hussars
The Cheshire Yeomanry (Earl of Chester's Hussars)
Royal 1st Devon Yeomanry (Hussars)
Royal North Devon Hussars Yeomanry
Dorset (Queen's Own) Yeomanry
Royal Gloucestershire Hussars, Yeomanry
Royal East Kent Yeomanry (The Duke of Connaught's Own Mounted
    Rifles)
Queen's Own West Kent Hussars
Lancashire Hussars
Leicestershire Yeomanry
1st County of London Yeomanry (Middlesex Duke of Cambridge's Hussars)
3rd County of London Yeomanry (Sharp shooters Hussars)
Northumberland Hussars
Nottinghamshire Yeomanry (Sherwood Rangers)
South Nottinghamshire Hussars
Queen's Own Oxfordshire Hussars
Pembroke Yeomanry
West Somerset Hussars
Staffordshire Yeomanry (Queen's Own Royal Regiment)
Suffolk Yeomanry (The Duke of York's Own Royal Suffolk Hussars)
Warwickshire Yeomanry
Welsh Horse Yeomanry
Westmorland and Cumberland Hussars
Royal Wiltshire Hussars (Prince of Wales's Own Royal Regiment)
Worcestershire Yeomanry (The Queen's Own Worcestershire Hussars)
Yorkshire Hussars (Alexandra, Princess of Wales' Own)

Imperial Camel Corps

Many of the Territorial Force units mentioned above, as well as some of the 6th Inniskilling Dragoons, served on foot, there being very little need for mounted troops in France after the battle of Mons in 1914. For this purpose pairs of Yeomanry regiments were combined to form one battalion of infantry and renamed. Listed following are the regiments involved and the battalions so formed. Some Yeomanry regiments, however, continued in their traditional cavalry role notably in the Middle East.

| Regiment of Cavalry | Infantry Battalion |
|---|---|
| 1/1st Royal Devon Yeomanry <br> 1/1st Royal North Devon Yeomanry | 16th (Royal 1st Devon & R. Nth Devon Yeo.) Battn. Devonshire Regt. |
| 1/1st West Somerset Yeomanry | 12th (West Somerset Yeo.) Battn. Somerset L.I. |
| 1/1st Fife and Forfar Yeomanry | 14th (Fife and Forfar Yeo.) Battn. Royal Highlanders |
| 1/1st Ayrshire Yeomanry <br> 1/1st Lanark Yeomanry | 12th (Ayr & Lanark Yeo.) Battn. Royal Scots Fusiliers |
| 1/1st East Kent Yeomanry <br> 1/1st West Kent Yeomanry | 10th (Royal East Kent and West Kent Yeo.) Battn. East Kent Regiment |
| 1/1st Sussex Yeomanry | 16th (Sussex Yeo.) Battn. Royal Sussex Regiment |
| 1/1st Suffolk Yeomanry | 15th (Suffolk Yeo.) Battn. Suffolk Regiment |
| 1/1st Norfolk Yeomanry | 12th (Norfolk Yeo.) Battn. Norfolk Regiment. |
| 1/1st Shropshire Yeomanry <br> 1/1st Cheshire Yeomanry | 10th (Shropshire & Cheshire Yeo.) Battn. Shropshire L.I. |
| 1/1st Denbigh Yeomanry | 24th (Denbigh Yeo.) Battn. Royal Welch Fusiliers |
| 1/1st Montgomery Yeomanry <br> 1/1st Welsh Horse Yeomanry. | 25th (Montgomery & Welsh Horse Yeo.) Battn Royal Welch Fusiliers |
| 1/1st Pembroke Yeomanry <br> 1/1st Glamorgan Yeomanry | 24th (Pembroke & Glamorgan Yeo.) Battn. Welch Regiment |
| 1/1st Lovat's Scouts Yeomanry | 10th (Lovat's Scouts) Battn. The Q.O. Cameron Highlanders |
| 1/1st Scottish Horse Yeomanry | 13th (Scottish Horse Battn. The Black Watch) Royal Highlanders |
| 2 Squadrons Glasgow Yeomanry | 18th (Glasgow Yeo.) Battn. Highland Light Infantry |
| 2 Squadrons Duke of Lancaster's Own Yeomanry | 12th (Duke of Lancaster's Own Yeo.) Battn. Manchester Regt. |
| 1/1 Yorkshire Hussars | 9th (Yorkshire Hussars) Battn. West Yorkshire Regt. |
| 2/1 Northumberland Hussars | 9th (Northumberland Hussars) Battn. Northumberland Fusiliers |
| 1/1 Lancashire Hussars | 18th(Lancashire Hussars) Battn. The King's (Liverpool Regiment) |
| 1 Squadron (Service) 6th Inniskilling Dragoons 'B' and 'C' Squadrons North Irish Horse | 9th (North Irish Horse) Battn. Royal Irish Fusiliers |
| 1/1 Hampshire Yeomanry | 15th (Hampshire Yeo.) Battn. Hampshire Regiment. |
| 1/1 Westmorland and Cumberland Yeomanry | 7th (Westmorland and Cumberland Yeomanry) Battn. Border Regiment |
| 1/1 Royal Wiltshire Yeomanry | 6th (Wiltshire Yeomanry) Battn. Wiltshire Regiment. |
| 1st South Irish Horse <br> 2nd South Irish Horse | 7th (South Irish Horse) Battn. Royal Irish Regiment. |

## ARTILLERY
Honourable Artillery Company
Royal Horse Artillery
Royal Field Artillery
Royal Garrison Artillery

## INFANTRY
### Foot Guards
Coldstream Guards
Scots Guards
Grenadier Guards
Irish Guards
Welsh Guards (formed 1915)
Guards Machine Gun Regiment

### Infantry Regiments
The Royal Scots
The Queen's (Royal West Surrey Regiment)
The Buffs (East Kent Regiment)
The King's Own (Royal Lancaster Regiment)
The Northumberland Fusiliers
The Royal Warwickshire Regiment
The Royal Fusiliers (City of London Regiment)
The King's (Liverpool Regiment)
The Norfolk Regiment
The Lincolnshire Regiment
The Devonshire Regiment
The Suffolk Regiment
Prince Albert's (Somerset Light Infantry)
The Prince of Wales's Own (West Yorkshire Regiment)
The East Yorkshire Regiment
The Bedfordshire Regiment
The Leicestershire Regiment
The Royal Irish Regiment
Alexandra, Princess of Wales's Own (Yorkshire Regiment)
  *(The Green Howards)*
The Lancashire Fusiliers
The Royal Scots Fusiliers

The Cheshire Regiment
The Royal Welsh Fusiliers
The South Wales Borderers
The King's Own Scottish Borderers
The Cameronians (Scottish Rifles)
The Royal Inniskilling Fusiliers
The Gloucestershire Regiment
The Worcestershire Regiment
The East Lancashire Regiment
The East Surrey Regiment
The Duke of Cornwall's Light Infantry
The Duke of Wellington's (West Riding Regiment)
The Border Regiment
The Royal Sussex Regiment
The Hampshire Regiment
The South Staffordshire Regiment
The Dorsetshire Regiment
The Prince of Wales's Volunteers (South Lancashire Regiment)
The Welsh Regiment
The Black Watch (Royal Highlanders)
The Oxfordshire and Buckinghamshire Light Infantry
The Essex Regiment
The Sherwood Foresters (Nottinghamshire and Derbyshire Regiment)
The Loyal North Lancashire Regiment
The Northamptonshire Regiment
Princess Charlotte of Wales's (Royal Berkshire Regiment)
The Queen's Own (Royal West Kent Regiment)
The King's Own (Yorkshire Light Infantry)
The King's (Shropshire Light Infantry)
The Duke of Cambridge's Own (Middlesex Regiment)
The King's Royal Rifle Corps ' 'The Green Jackets'
The Duke of Edinburgh's (Wiltshire Regiment)
The Manchester Regiment
The Prince of Wales's (North Staffordshire Regiment)
The York and Lancaster Regiment
The Durham Light Infantry
The Highland Light Infantry
Seaforth Highlanders (Ross-shire, Buffs, The Duke of Albany's)

The Gordon Highlanders
The Queen's Own Cameron Highlanders
The Royal Irish Rifles
Princess Victoria's (Royal Irish Fusiliers)
The Connaught Rangers
Princess Louise's (Argyll and Sutherland Highlanders)
The Prince of Wales's Leinster Regiment (Royal Canadians)
The Royal Munster Fusiliers
The Royal Dublin Fusiliers
The Rifle Brigade (The Prince Consort's Own)

## Territorial Force Regiments
Honourable Artillery Company (Infantry)
The Royal Monmouthshire Royal Engineers
The London Regiment
Inns of Court Officers Training Corps
The Monmouthshire Regiment
The Cambridgeshire Regiment
The Hertfordshire Regiment
The Herefordshire Regiment
Army Cyclist Corps formed from:
    The Northern Cyclist Battalion
    The Highland Cyclist Battalion
    The Kent Cyclist Battalion
    The Huntingdonshire Cyclist Battalion
    and 9 other TF Cyclist Battalions.
The Royal Jersey Militia
The Royal Guernsey Light Infantry

## CORPS
Corps of Royal Engineers
Royal Defence Corps
Army Service Corps
Royal Army Medical Corps
Labour Corps
Royal Army Ordnance Corps
Royal Army Veterinary Corps
Royal Army Pay Corps

Corps of Army Schoolmasters
Corps of Military Mounted Police
Corps of Military Foot Police
Corps of the Small Arms School
Military Provost Staff Corps
Non-Combatant Corps
Queen Mary's Army Auxiliary Corps
Machine Gun Corps
Tank Corps

The following units also existed and were mostly not regiments but had
    separate badges:
Isle of Man Volunteers
First Aid Nursing Yeomanry
Queen Alexandra's Imperial Military Nursing Service
Chaplains Department
Army Service Corps Armoured Car Convoys
Army Remount Service
Army Scripture Readers
Forage Corps (for Women) formed 1916
Many Military Schools and Officers Training Corps
Royal Navy Brigade - later RN Division. Consisted of the following:
    Drake, Hawke, Benbow, Collingwood, Nelson, Howe, Hood, Anson,
    and the Machine Gun Battalion.
Prisoner of War Companies
Military Prisons

A fuller list can be found in Ref. 30.

# APPENDIX II

## THE ARMY 1914-18: A List of Divisions

### The Regular Army
The Guards Division
1st- 8th Divisions and the 27th, 28th, 29th Divisions.

### New Army Divisions
9th-26th and 30th-41st Divisions
43rd, 44th and 45th served only in India.
The 30th -35th Divisions were formed to found the 4th Army in the early days of the war. This army was disbanded and re-formed in April 1915. The composition of the Divisions was also changed at the same time.

### Territorial Force Divisions
42nd-69th except 63rd Division.

### Other Divisions
63rd (Royal Naval)
(Note: 70th Division was never formed.)
71st, 72nd, 73rd Home Service Divisions.
74th formed at El Arish from all British units of dismounted yeomanry.
75th formed at El Arish from some Indian units.

### Cavalry Divisions
1st, 2nd and 3rd (4th and 5th were the old 1st and 2nd Indian Cavalry Divisions).

### Other Mounted Divisions
1st, 2nd, 2nd/2nd, and 4th Mounted Divisions formed from Yeomanry. Mounted Yeomanry Division. Also 1st-5th Australian; 1st-4th Canadian; New Zealand; Portuguese 1st and 2nd.

Except where listed below, the above Divisions served only in France after sailing from England.

| 1st Mounted | | | 71st | | |
|---|---|---|---|---|---|
| 2nd/2nd Mounted | } | Served in England only | 72nd | } | Served in England only |
| 4th Mounted | | | 73rd | | |
| 43rd | | | 64th | | |
| 44th | } | Served in India only | 65th | | |
| 45th | | | 67th | } | Served in England only |
| | | | 68th | | |
| | | | 69th | | |

The following divisions spent some time in the countries named as well as France.

| | | | | | |
|---|---|---|---|---|---|
| 42nd | | | 13th | Mesopotamia | |
| * 46th | (sailed but recalled) | | 45th | Mesopotamia (part) | |
| * 31st | | Egypt | | | |
| * 11th | | 1914- | 52nd | | |
| * 29th | | June | 54th | (Not France) | |
| 52nd | | 1917 | 74th | | Pales-tine |
| 53rd | | includes | 75th | (Not France) | June 1917–1918 |
| 54th | (Not France) | units in | 53rd | (Not France) | |
| 2nd | Mounted Division | transit | 60th | (Not France) | |
| * 63rd | (Royal Naval) | marked* | 10th | (Not France) | |
| * 10th | (Not France) | | | many assorted | |
| * 13th | (Not France) | | | mounted units | |
| 74th | | | | | |
| 75th | (Not France) | | 48th | | |
| | | | 41st | | |
| 16th | (Not France | | 23rd | | Italy |
| 22nd | | Salonika | 7th | | |
| 26th | | (Greece) | 5th | | |
| 27th | | to June | | | Mace-donia |
| 28th | | 1917 | 22nd | | Greece |
| 60th | (Not France) | | 26th | | Bul-garia. |
| | | | 27th | | |
| 10th | (Not France) | | 28th | | |
| 11th | | | | | |
| 29th | | Gallipoli | 10th Div. | Russia — not France | |
| 42nd | | Helles | | | |
| 52nd | | Sulva | | | |
| 53rd | | Mudros | 59th | Ireland | |
| 54th | | (on Lemnos) | | | |
| 27th | | | | | |
| 28th | | | | | |
| Royal Naval (63rd) | | | | | |
| 13th | (Not France) | | | | |
| 2nd Mounted | (dismantled) | | | | |

In addition to the usual numbers some divisions were given names. These should not be confused with Battalion names, although the method of indicating Territorial Divisions was similar to that used for Territorial Battalions. (see page 15)

| | |
|---|---|
| 9th Div. Scottish | 48th Div. 1/1st South Midland |
| 11th Div. Northern | 49th Div. 1/1st West Riding |
| 12th Div. Eastern | 50th Div. 1/1st Northumbrian |
| 15th Div. Scottish | 51st Div. Highland |
| 16th Div. Irish | 55th Div. 1/1st West Lancashire |
| 17th Div. Northern | 56th Div. 1/1st London |
| 18th Div. Eastern | 57th Div. 2nd West Ham |
| 19th Div. Western | 58th Div. 2/1st London |
| 20th Div. Light | 59th Div. 2nd North Midland |
| 30th Div. Ulster | 60th Div. 2/2nd London |
| 38th Div. Welsh | 61st Div. 2nd South Midland |
| 42nd Div. 1st East Lancashire | 62nd Div. 2nd West Riding |
| 46th Div. 1st North Midland | 63rd Div. Royal Naval |
| 47th Div. 1/2nd London | 66th Div. 2nd East Lancashire |

# APPENDIX III

## THE BRITISH FORCES IN FRANCE

### 1916

As well as infantry, cavalry and artillery the British Army had many other types of unit. A list of some of the various types for July 1916 is given below. By the end of the war a few others had been added and in some cases command or allocation of units had been transferred. The list is by no means complete but it gives an idea of the variety of units. The numbers in the left-hand column give a rough idea of the total number of units of that type in France.

### Units directly under GHQ

These were often allocated to one of the four (later five) armies but they reported to GHQ There were also lines of communication troops which served all five armies.

| Total No. of Units in France | Type of Unit | Name of Corps |
|---|---|---|
| | GHQ Wireless Signal Company | RE |
| 22 | Searchlight Sections | RA |
| 91 | Sound Ranging Companies | RA |
| | Anti Aircraft Artillery | RA |
| 5 | Special Battalion (Gas) | RE |
| | Special Works Park (Camouflage) | RE |
| | Wireless Depot | RE |
| | Wireless School | RE |
| 42 | Ordnance Companies | ROC |
| | Base Camouflage Works | RE |
| | GHQ Troop Company | RE |
| | Army Post Office | RE (later APS) |
| | Base Stationery Depot | RE |
| | Publications Department | RE |
| | Army Printing Depot | RE |

| Total No. of Units in France | Type of Unit | Name of Corps |
|---|---|---|
| | Printing and Photography Company | RE |
| | Rubber Stamp Factory | RE |
| | Typewriter Repair Service | RE |
| 5 | Supply Depots | ROC |
| 41 | Ambulance Trains (2 types) | RAMC |
| 80 | Hospitals (several types) | RAMC |
| 26 | Mobile Labs (4 types) | RAMC |
| 16 | Convalescent Homes | RAMC |
| 5 | Supply Depots (medical) | RAMC |
| 19 | Supply Depots | ASC |
| 45 | Field Bakeries | ASC |
| 58 | Bakery Sections | ASC |
| 29 | Field Butchers | ASC |
| 10 | Remount Depot (horse replacements) | ASC |
| 1 | Training School | ASC |
| 5 | Ambulance Flotilla (barges) | RAMC and RE |
| | War Dog Training School | RE |
| 24 | Veterinary Hospitals | AVC |
| 18 | Veterinary Evacuating Sec. | AVC |
| 2 | Veterinary Stores | AVC |
| 1 | Veterinary Laboratory | AVC |
| 1 | Veterinary Disposal Branch | AVC |
| | Ordnance Base Work Shop | ROC |
| | Messenger Dog Section | RE |
| 12 | Infantry Labour Battalions | Formed from Infantry Regts. |
| 11 | Labour Corps Companies | LC |
| 8 | Non-combatant Companies | |
| 30 | Labour Companies | ASC |
| 3 | Labour Companies | Naval |
| 2 | Railway Companies | ASC |
| 73 | Railway Supply Detachments | ASC |
| 5 | Auxiliary (Petrol) Companies | ASC |
| | Auxiliary (Bus) Company | ASC |
| | Auxiliary (Steam) Company | ASC |

| Total No. of Units in France | Type of Unit | Name of Corps |
|---|---|---|
| | Auxiliary (Water) Company | ASC |
| 84 | Depot Units of Supply | ASC |
| | Advance Park Company | RE |
| | Base Park Company | RE |
| 4 | Field Survey Companies | RE |
| 4 | Artisan Work Companies | RE |
| 38 | Lines of Communication Supply Companies | ASC |

## Army Troops

Units under the control of an Army were termed Army Troops and could consist of the following.

| Total No. of Units in France | Type of Unit | Name of Corps | Total per Army |
|---|---|---|---|
| | Special (Projector) Companies (Gas) | RE | 3 |
| | Special (Mortar) Companies | RE | 1 |
| | Advanced Parks | RE | 2 |
| 51 | Army Troops Companies | RE | 16 |
| 6 | Siege Companies | RE | 2 |
| 25 | Tunnelling Companies | RE | 8 |
| | Electrical & Mechanical Company | RE | 1 |
| | Boring Section | RE | 1 |
| | Army Workshop | RE | 1 |
| | Sound Ranging Sections | RE | 7 |
| | Observation Groups | RE | 7 |
| | Anti-Aircraft Searchlight Sections | RE | 6 |
| | Foreway Company (in charge of tramways etc. in defended zones) | RE | 1 |
| | Airline Sections | RE | 3 |
| | Cable Sections | RE | 2 |
| | Light Railway Signal Section | RE | 1 |
| | Signal Construction Section | RE | 1 |
| | Tunnelling School | RE | 1 |

| Total No. of Units in France | Type of Unit | Name of Corps | Total per Army |
|---|---|---|---|
| | Mining Companies | RE | 1 |
| | Mine Rescue School | RE | 1 |
| | Field Survey Company | RE | 1 |
| | Artisan Work Company | RE | 1 |
| | Motor Mobile Lofts for pigeons | 4 | |
| | Horse Drawn Mobile Lofts for pigeons | 12 | |
| | Fixed Loft for pigeons | 1 | |
| | Garrison Guard Company | 1 | |
| | Military Police Traffic Control | | squadron 1, company 1 |
| | Auxiliary Companies | ASC | 3 |
| | Pontoon Parks, M.T. Companies | ASC | 2 |
| | Army Troops, M.T. Companies | ASC | 3 |
| | Mobile Repair Unit | ASC | 1 |
| | Siege Battery Transport | ASC | 2 |
| | Water Tank Company | ASC | 1 |
| 31 | Motor Ambulance Convoys | ASC and RAMC | 5 |
| 60 | Casualty Clearing Stations | RAMC | 10 |
| 18 | Advanced Depots Medical Stores | RAMC | 2 |
| 25 | Mobile Laboratories | RAMC | 5 |
| 5 | Mobile Dental Units | RAMC | 1 |
| | Stationary Hospital | RAMC | 1 |
| | Sanitary Sections | RAMC | 15 |
| 5 | X-Ray Units | RAMC | 1 |
| | Heavy Mobile Workshop | ROC | 1 |
| | Light Mobile Workshops | ROC | 2 |
| | Ordnance Gun Park | ROC | 1 |
| | Officers' Clothing Depot | ROC | 1 |
| | Forestry Companies | RE | 3 |
| | Labour Companies (British) | | 60 |
| | Area Employment Companies | | 8 |
| | Area Employment (Garrison Guard) Companies | | 5 |
| | Italian Labour Companies | | 34 |
| | Prisoner of War Companies | | 25 |

| Total No. of Units in France | Type of Unit | Name of Corps | Total per Army |
|---|---|---|---|
| | Indian Labour Companies | 11 | |
| | Chinese Labour Companies | 10 | |
| | Army Printing & Stationery Services Section | | 1 |
| | RHA Army Section | RA | 1 |
| | RFA Army Brigade | RA | 23 |
| | RGA Army Brigade | RA | 22 |
| | RGA Siege Batteries | RA | 15 |
| | AA Batteries | RA | 4 |
| | AA Workshop | ASC | 1 |
| | Cavalry Divisions | 1 | |
| | Barge Filtration Unit | RE | 1 |
| | Advanced Photographic Section | RE | 1 |

Similarly, Corps Troops could consist of:

| | Name of Corps | Units per Corps |
|---|---|---|
| A regiment of cavalry | 1 | |
| Cyclist Battalion | 1 | |
| Motor Machine Gun Battery | MGC | 1 |
| Corps Signal Company | RE | 1 |
| ASC Heavy Artillery (Transport) Company | ASC | 1 |
| Supply Columns (1 for each Division) | ASC | 4 or 5 |
| Mobile Ordnance Workshops | ROC | 2 |
| Corps Ammunition Park | ASC | 1 |
| Heavy Artillery Groups | RA | 2 |
| Army Troop Companies | RE | 2 |
| Tunnelling Company | RE | |
| Royal Flying Corps | RFC | |
| Special Works Park (Camouflage) | RE | 1 |
| Field Cashier | APC | |
| Ordnance Officer and Staff | | |
| Postal Service Detachment | | |
| Army Chaplains Department | | |
| Veterinary Units | | |

Plus any Army Troops allocated to the Corps.

Likewise, Divisional Troops

| | Name of Corps | Units per Division | |
|---|---|---|---|
| Cavalry Squadron | 1 | | |
| Cyclist Company | 1 | | |
| Batteries Artillery | RA | 16(64 Guns) | |
| Trench Mortar Batteries | RA | 3 | |
| Field Company Engineers | RE | 3 | |
| Signal Company | RE | 1 | |
| Pioneer Battalion | | 1 | |
| Company of Divisional Train (Horse) | ASC | 4 | |
| Field Ambulances | RAMC | 3 | |
| Sanitary Section | RE | 1 | |
| Mobile Veterinary Section | AVC | 1 | |
| Infantry Labour Battalion | | 1 | |
| Field Ambulance Workshop (up to April 1916) | ASC | | 1 |
| Ordnance Officers | | 5 | |
| Chaplains | 17 | | |
| Post services | APS | 1 | |
| Machine Gun Company (formed April 1917) | MGC | 1 | |

Plus any Corps Troop units allocated to the Division.

The complement of all ranks in a division varied during the War but was around 18,000. Similarly, the number of guns varied in size and number. A typical breakdown of numbers would be

    infantry 12,000
    artillery 4,000
    others 2,000.

A battalion would have about 32 officers and 992 other ranks. Within a battalion, of which there were 12 per division (reduced to 9 in January 1918), there would be

1 Signal Section - part of the RE Company

Cooks  
Sanitary Section  
Stretcher Bearers  
Transport Drivers     }   Total about 200 supplied by  
  mostly handcarts       the battalion from its own men  
and wagons  
Bandsmen

RAMC officer in Regimental Aid Post.

## Army Service Corps
ASC Motor Transport Companies 605
ASC Horse Transport Companies 552
ASC Mobile Repair Depots  22
ASC Mobile Depots  21

## Royal Engineers
The Royal Engineers had 77 different types of unit (many shown above).
The total of all RE units was 531.

# APPENDIX IV

## A List of the Battles involving British Troops in France and Belgium

A more expansive list can be found in A.F. Becke's *Order of Battle of Divisions*. A list of actions which took place during the period covered by each volume is given in *The Official History* series. The battles have names defined by the Historical Section of the Committee of Imperial Defence London and printed in their book *Principal Events 1914-18*, HMSO. A copy is to be found in WO161/102 at the PRO and a second copy with annotations of participating units is in WO161 /103. This was reprinted by the London Stamp Exchange, 1988.

### 1914

| | |
|---|---|
| **23rd August** | **Battle of Mons** |
| 1st September | Fighting at Compiegne. |
| **6th-9th September** | **Battle of the Marne** |
| **14th-28th September** | **Battle of the Aisne** |
| 18th September-16th October | Battle of Flanders |
| 13th October-2nd November | Battle of Armentiers |
| 13th October | Capture of Meteren |
| **12th October-17th November** | **1st Battle of Ypres** |
| 18th-23rd December | Battle of Givenchy |

### 1915

| | |
|---|---|
| 23rd February | Capture of Trench at Givenchy |
| **10th-2th March** | **Battle of Neuve-Chapelle** |
| 17th April | Capture of Hill 60 |
| 22nd April-14th May | 2nd Battle of Ypres |
| 15th-5th May | Battle of Festubert |
| rd June | Gain at Givenchy |
| 9th August | Capture of Trench near Hooge |
| **25th September** | **5th October Battle of Loos and Champagne** |
| 25th September | Bois Grenier |

## 1916

| | |
|---|---|
| 27th March-16th April | Fighting at St Eloi |
| 21st May | German Attack on Vimy Ridge |
| **1st July-18th November** | **Battles of the Somme** |

During this period many actions were fought. They included

| | |
|---|---|
| 1st-13th July | Battle of Albert |
| 2nd-4th July | Capture of la Boiselle |
| 10th July | Capture of Contalmaison |
| 14th-17th July | Battle of Bazentin Ridge |
| 15th July-3rd | September Battle of Delville Wood |
| 20th-25th July | Attack on High Wood |
| 23rd July-3rd September | Battle of Pozieres Ridge |
| 3rd-6th September | Battle of Guillemont |
| 9th September | Battle of Ginchy |
| 2nd-22nd September | Battle of Flers-Courcelette |
| 15th September | Capture of Martinpuich |
| 26th-28th September | Battle of Thiepval |
| 25th-28th September | Battle of Morval |
| 1st-8th October | Battle of Transloy Ridges |
| 1st-3rd October | Capture of Eaucourt l'abbaye |
| 7th October | Capture of Le Sars |
| 7th October-5th November | Attacks on Butte de Warlencourt |
| 3rd-11th November | Battle of the Ancre Heights |
| 13th-18th November | Battle of the Ancre |

## 1917

| | |
|---|---|
| 7th January | Raid south of Armentiers |
| 23rd January | Raid at Neuville |
| 29th January | Raid at Butte de Warlencourt |
| 7th February | Capture of Grandecourt |
| **23rd February-5th April** | **German Retreat to the Hindenburg Line** |
| 23rd February | Fighting near Gueudecourt |
| 24th February | Capture of Petit Miraumont |
| 26th February | Capture of Le Barque |
| 28th February | Capture of Gommecourt |
| 10th March | Capture of Irles |
| 17th March | Capture of Bapaume |
| 18th March | Capture of Peronne |

| | |
|---|---|
| **9th April-3rd May** | **Battle of Arras** |
| 9th-14th April 1st | Battle of the Scarpe |
| **9th-14th April** | **Battle of Vimy Ridge** |
| 23rd-24th April | 2nd Battle of the Scarpe |
| 28th-29th April | Battle of Arleux |
| 3rd-4th May 3rd | Battle of the Scarpe |
| 16th April-9th May | 2nd Battle of the Aisne (mostly French) |
| 13th-16th May | Capture of Roeux |
| **7th-14th June** | **Battle of Messines** |
| 1st July | Attack on Lievin |
| 15th-25th August | Battle of Hill 70, Lens |
| **31st July-10th November** | **Battle of Ypres (3rd Ypres)** |
| 31st July-2nd August | Battle of Pilckem Ridge |
| 16th-18th August | Battle of Lanemarck |
| 19th August | The Cockcroft |
| 22nd August | Fighting in front of St Julien |
| 22nd-25th September | Battle of Menin Road Bridge |
| 26th-30th September | Battle of Polygon Wood |
| 4th October | Battle of Broodseinde |
| 9th October | Battle of Poelcappelle |
| **12th October** | **1st Battle of Passchendaele** |
| **26th October-2nd November** | **2nd Battle of Passchendaele** |
| **20th November-3rd December** | **Battle of Cambrai** |
| 20th-21st November | The Tank Attack |
| 21st November | Recapture of Noyelles |
| 23rd-28th November | Capture of Bourlon Wood |
| 30th November-3rd December | The German Counter Attacks |
| 30th November | Attack on Gouzeaucourt |
| 1st December | Attack on Villers Guislain and Gauche Wood |
| 30th December | Welch Ridge |

## 1918

| | |
|---|---|
| **21st March-4th April** | **1st Battle of the Somme** |
| 21st-23rd March | Battle of St Quentin |
| 24th-25th March | Action of the Somme Crossing |
| 24th-25th March | 1st Battle of Bapaume |

**1918** (*continued*)

| | |
|---|---|
| 28th March | 1st Battle of Arras |
| 26th-27th March | Battle of Rosieres |
| 5th April | Battle of the Avre |
| 28th June | La Becque |
| **9th-29th April** | **Battles of the Lys** |
| 9th-11th April | Battles of Estaires |
| 12th-15th April | Battles of Hazebrouck |
| 13th-15th April | Defence of Hinges Ridge |
| 13th-15th April | Battle of Bailleul |
| 9th-17th April | 1st Defence of Givenchy |
| 17th-19th April | 1st Battle of Kemmel Ridge |
| 18th April | Battle of Bethune |
| 12th-15th April | Defence of the Nieppe Forest |
| 18th-19th April | 2nd Defence of Givenchy |
| 25th-26th April | 2nd Battle of Kemmel Ridge |
| 29th April | Battle of Scherpenberg |
| **20th-31st July** | **Battles of the Marne** |
| 20th-31st July | Battle of Tardenois |
| 20th-31st July | Fighting in the Andre Valley |
| **24th Augus-3rd September** | **2nd Battle of the Somme** |
| 21st-23rd August | Battle of Albert |
| 24th August | Capture of Mory Copse |
| 25th August | Capture of Belagnies and Sapignies |
| 31st August-3rd September | 2nd Battle of Bapaume |
| **5th August-18th September** | **The Advance in Flanders** |
| 5th-11th August | Battle of Amiens |
| 18th August | Capture of Outtersteene Ridge |
| 18th August | Capture of Hoegennacker Ridge |
| 24th August | Capture of Givenchy Craters |
| 1st September | Capture of Neuve Eglise |
| 2nd September | Capture of Wulverghem |
| 4th September | Capture of Ploegsteert and Hill 63 |
| 17th September | Capture of Canteleux Trench |
| **26th August-3rd September** | **2nd Battle of Arras** |
| 26th-30th August | Battle of the Scarpe |
| 3rd September | Assault of the Drocourt-Queant Line |
| **18th September-9th October** | **Battles of the Hindenburg Line** |

| | |
|---|---|
| 12th September | Battle of Havrincourt |
| 18th September | Battle of Epehy |
| 21st September | The Knoll |
| 24th September | Attack on Quadrilateral and Fresnoy |
| 27th September | Battle of the Canal du Nord |
| 29th September | Passage at Bellenglise |
| 29th September-1st October | Battle of the St Quentin Canal |
| 1st October | Capture of Mont sur l'Oeuvre |
| 3rd-5th October | Battle of Beaurevoir Line |
| 8th-9th October | Battle of Cambrai |
| 8th October | Capture of Forenville |
| 8th October | Capture of Niergnies |
| 9th October | Capture of Cambrai |

## The Final Advance
## 1918
### 17th October-11th November in Picardy

| | |
|---|---|
| 20th October | Capture of Solesmes |
| 23rd October | Capture of Grand Champ Ridge |
| 23rd October | Capture of Bousies |
| 17th-25th October | Battle of the Selle |
| 23rd October | Attack on Forest and Ovillers |
| 1st & 2nd November | Battle of Valenciennes |
| 1st November | Capture of Mont Houy |
| 2nd November | Attack S.W. of Landrecies |
| 4th November | Battle of the Sambre |
| | Capture of Le Quesnoy |
| 5th-7th November | Passage of the Grand Honnelle |
| 9th November | Occupation of Maubeuge |

### 2nd October-11th November in Artois

| | |
|---|---|
| 7th-8th October | Forcing the Rouvroy-Fresne Line |
| 17th October | Capture of Douai |
| 17th October | Occupation of Lille |
| 11th November | Capture of Mons |

### 28th September-11th November in Flanders

| | |
|---|---|
| 28th September-2nd November | Battle of Ypres |
| 14th-19th October | Battle of Courtrai |
| 25th October | Ooteghem |
| 31st October | Tieghem |

## SOME ACTIONS OUTSIDE FRANCE*

| | |
|---|---|
| 8th August 1914-1st December 1917 | British in German East Africa |
| 20th August 1914-18th February 1916 | British in Cameroons |
| 19th September 1914-9th July 1915 | British in German S.W. Africa |
| 3rd-21st November 1914 | British in Suez and Akaba |
| 11th-17th November 1914 | Mesopotamia |
| 1st January 1915-31st December 1917 | British in British East Africa |
| 19th February-19th March 1915 | British attack Dardanelles |
| 17th April-28th September 1915 | Tigris - Kut al Amara |
| 23rd April 1915-9th January 1916 | British in Gallipoli |
| 8th August 1915 | Anzacs at Sulva Bay |
| 5th October 1915-November 1918 | British in Salonika |
| 11th-22nd November 1915 | River Euphrates |
| 25th November 1915-29th April 1916 | British under siege in Kut |
| 5th-12th August 1916 | British advance into Sinai |
| 13th December 1916-3rd April 1917 | Fighting in Kut and Baghdad |
| 1st January 1917-20th March 1917 | British advance into Palestine |
| 21st July-28th September 1917 | British Forces at River Euphrates |
| 7th October-7th November 1917 | Battle of Gaza |
| 5th November-9th December 1917 | British capture Jerusalem |
| 7th November 1917-1st March 1918 | British Forces in Italy |
| 3rd December 1917-23rd October 1918 | British in Mesopotamia |
| 1st January-30th September 1918 | British advance along River Jordan |
| 3rd April-31st December 1918 | British Forces in Russia |

* The dates given refer to battles or periods of action and not to the length of time that British troops remained in the area.

## FACTS

1. Howard White HOLDING, M2/153147 Private ASC (taken from medal still in family).
2. Awarded British War Medal and Victory Medal - Medal Office.
3. Was at one time Lance Corporal - photo with stripe. Fig.10.
4. Wears on lower left arm single inverted stripe (photo).
5. Wears on lower right arm small inverted triple stripe (photo).
6. Earliest known army service - 25th February 1916 (Postcard - UK Postmark) Fig.9.
7. Earliest known army service in France - 18th June 1916(Card from France). Fig.11.
8. Latest known army service - in Brussels - (27th April)? 1919. Postcard with Belgian postmark. (Almost unreadable.)
9. Only known locations
   NAMUR - 12th February 1919 (photo), Fig.12.
   WATERLOO - en route to Brussels 27th April ? 1919 (Postcard).
These may have been taken during 'educational visits' after the 1918 Armistice prior to demob and hence not true postings.
10. Two group photographs.
    (a) Taken in England while under training and before 25th February 1916, showing 10 men (including a Sergeant) in a workshop. (Postcard as 6.)
    (b) Taken outside a German Horse Hospital on 12th February 1919 in NAMUR showing 13 men. Besides my father, one other (possibly 2) men appear in both photos. (Same photo as 9.) Fig.12.
11. He was a trained apprenticed railway enginefitter and just prior to call-up a lorry design draughtsman and he may have worked on the buses as a fitter.

## UNSUBSTANTIATED FACTS AND TRADITIONS

12. He was a vehicle fitter in the Army (remembered as being on lost discharge papers).
13. He worked on ambulances - vague memories of relatives.
14. He was stationed near Albert at Christmas 1916 or 1917 (picture postcard sent at Christmas shows view of Albert).
15. He served only in Northern Europe - vague memory.
16. He was twice mentioned in despatches (remembered as being on lost discharge papers).
17. He was once in Amiens (remembered inscription in French bible - now lost).
18. He was to go to Germany in the Army of Occupation but in the end did not go. (Comment from his girlfriend who was glad that he did not go.)

Fig. 1. Information relating to Private Howard White Holding.

## ASSUMPTIONS FROM FIG. 1

A. He served in a motor transport workshop with the ASC (Facts 1, 10, 11, 12).
B. As he was with a workshop, the unit would remain intact throughout the war except for traceable transfers and amalgamations. (Far behind the line and therefore few casualties.) Dangerous assumptions but no alternative with the limited data available.
C. He went overseas between 28th Feb. (Fact 6 says *on leave until noon 28th Feb*.) and 18th June 1916 (Fact 7). As leave was most likely to be embarkation leave, date of sailing is at the beginning of March rather than at any other time.
D. He was at Namur on 12th Feb. 1919 (Facts 9 and 10). The men look too untidy to be far from the camp.
E. He may have been near Albert at Christmas 1916 or 1917 (Fact 14).
F. He may have worked on ambulances (Fact 13).


## DEDUCTIONS FROM FIG.1

i. About 60 ASC Motor Transport Units left England between the two dates. (From monthly returns, war diaries and allocation lists in WO95/5494.)
ii. About 76 ASC Motor Transport Units could have been in Namur area in Feb. 1919. (GHQ Order of Battle, war diaries, Becke.)
iii. Only six units are in both lists - only two of these had ambulances - both MACs. An MAC Workshop had only 12 men (see Fact 10).
iv. No. 24 MAC did not go near Albert.
v. No. 21 MAC was within 3½ miles of Albert at Christmas 1916.
vi. Assume No. 21 MAC is ancestor's unit.
vii. Both No. 21 and No. 24 MACs left UK in early March 1916.
viii. Proof: ancestor's name is in the No. 21 MAC War Diary (an extra and unexpected bonus).

Fig. 2. Information obtained from Fig. 1

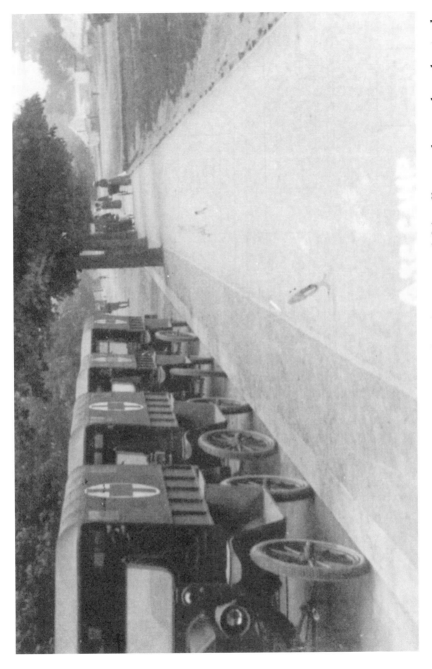

Figure 3. Views of army camps in the UK can be found at postcard fairs, flea markets and car boot sales. The picture shows a typical card depicting the ancestor's camp.

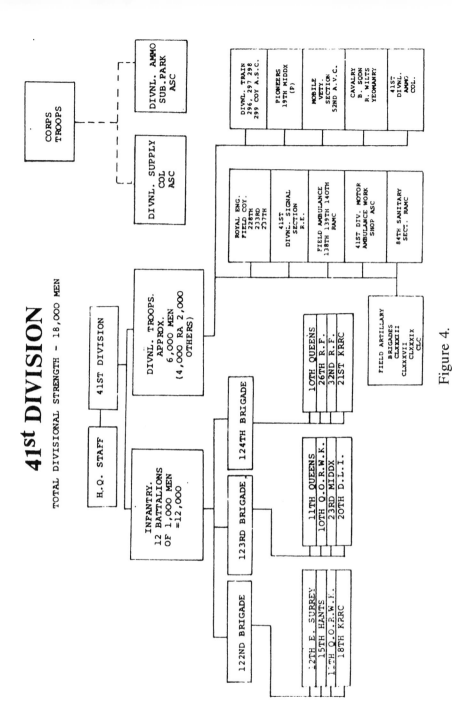

# 41st DIVISION

TOTAL DIVISIONAL STRENGTH - 18,000 MEN

Figure 4.

# ARMY ORGANISATION

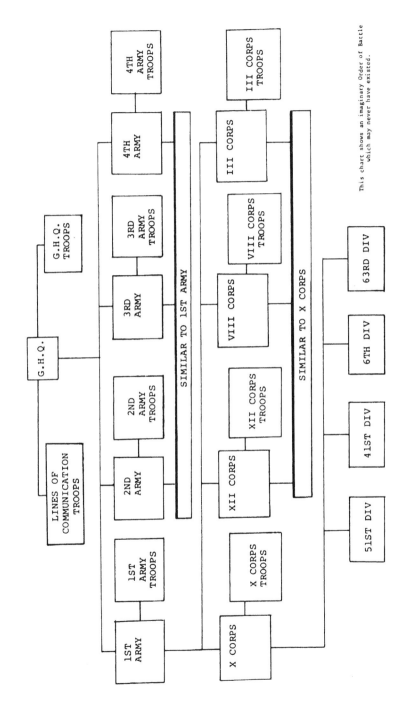

This chart shows an imaginary Order of Battle which may never have existed.

Figure 5.

# EXTRACT OF THE ENTRY FOR THE 41ST DIVISION IN BECKE'S ORDER OF BATTLE

Showing the type of information given in the tables and footnotes as at April 1916 at which time the Division was in England. The book repeats the information with appropriate footnotes at approximately 6 monthly intervals.

| Brigades | Battalions | Mounted Troops | Field Artillery Brigades [8] | Batteries |
|---|---|---|---|---|
| 122 | [3] 12/E. Surr.,15/Hants., 11/QORWK,18/KRRC | [6,14] B. Sqdn. R Wilts Yeo. | CLXXXIII(H) | [9] A(H) B(H) C(H) D(H) [16] |
| 123 | [2,4] 11/Queens, 10/QORWK , 23/Middx., 20/DLI [4] | | CLXXXVII | A B C D [17] |
| 124 | [2,5] 10/Queens, 26R.F., 32/R.F., 21KRCC | [7,15] 41st Div. Cyclist Coy | CLXXXIX  CXC | A B C D [18]  A B C D [19] |

| | Field Coy-Engineers | Divisional Signal Section | Pioneers |
|---|---|---|---|
| 122 | 228th [9] | | |
| 123 | 233rd [9] | 41st [9] | 19/Middx [10] (P) |
| 124 | 234th [9] | | |

| Brigades | Brigade Amm. Colns. | Divisional Amm.Coln. |
|---|---|---|
| 122 | CLXXXIII (H) BAC | |
| 123 | CLXXXVII BAC | 41st D.A.C. [8] |
| 124 | CLXXXIX BAC / CXC BAC | |

| | Mobile Vety.Sect. | Divnl. Train |
|---|---|---|
| 122 | | |
| 123 | 52nd [12] | 41st [13] |
| 124 | | |

| Field Ambulances | |
|---|---|
| 122 | 138 [11] |
| 123 | 139 [11] |
| 124 | 140 [11] |

Figure 6.

1. Formed at Aldershot in September 1915 as 41st Division. This was a new formation.
2. The infantry brigades. raised in 1915 as the 122nd, 123rd and 124th Bdes. were new formations.
3. The battalions were designated Bermondsey, 2nd Portsmouth, Lewisham, and Arts and Crafts. On 16 Oct 1915, 11/Q.O.R.W.K. joined 122nd Bde. from 118th Bde., 39th Div.
4. The battalions were designated Lambeth, Kent County, 2nd Football, and Wearside. On 16 Oct 1915, 10/Q.O.R.W.K. joined 123rd Bde. from 118th Bde., 39th Div.
5. The battalions were designated Battersea, Bankers, East Ham, and Yeomen Rifles.
6. Squadron joined the division 20.Nov 191515 at Aldershot. The squadron disembarked at Le Havre on 6 May 1916.
7. Company was formed in the division before 20 Nov 1915 at Aldershot. The company disembarked at Le Havre on 6 May 1916.
8. The artillery brigades were designated Hampstead, Fulham, Hackney, and Wimbledon. The D.A.C. was designated West Ham. The brigades were raised as 4-battery brigades; in each brigade the batteries were lettered A, B, C, and D, and each battery was a 4-gun battery. The divisional artillery disembarked at Le Havre between the 2nd and the 5th of May 1916.
9. The 3 field companies were designated Barnsley, Ripon, and Reading; the company designated Glasgow. The companies disembarked at Le Havre between 2nd and 6th May 1916.
10. The Pioneer Battalion was designated 2nd Public Works and it joined the division at Aldershot before 20 Nov 1915. The brigade disembarked at Le Havre on 2.5.16.
11. The 3 field ambulances were trained at Crookham; they went to France with the division and disembarked at Le Havre between the 3rd and 6th May 1916.
12. The section joined the division at Aldershot before 20 Nov 1915; it disembarked at Le Havre on 5 May 1916.
13. The train consisted of 296, 297, 298, and 299 Cos. A.S.C. It formed at Mytchett, went to France with the division and disembarked at Le Havre between the 2nd and 5th May 1916.
14. Squadron left the division on 31 May 1916, was attached to 2nd. Cavalry Division from 1st to 21st June 1916 and joined IX Corps Cavalry Regiment on 22.Jun 1916.
15. Company left the division on 28 May 1916 and joined II Corps Cyclist Bn. that day.
16. On 27 May 1916, A(H), B(H), and C(H) left CLXXXIII and became D(H)/CLXXXIX, D(H)/CLXXXVII, and D(H)/CXC; and D/CLXXXVII, and D/CXC joined and became A, B, and C/CLXXXIII; D(H) remained D(H)/CLXXXIII.
17. On 27 May 1916, D left and became B/CLXXXIII; and B(H)/CLXXXIII joined and became D(H)/CLXXXVII.
18. On 27 May 1916, D left and became A/CLXXXIII; and A(H)/CLXXXIII joined and became D(H)/CLXXXIX.
19. On 27 May 1916, D left and became C/CLXXXIII; and C(H)/CLXXXIII joined and became D(H)/CXC.

Fig. 7. Notes on Fig. 6.

Fig. 8. An unusual page from a War Diary showing the names of eight men. The line for 10th April 1919 is more typical of the usual daily entry. The unit was a small one (fewer than 170 men) and at the time of the entry was in the charge of the most junior of the eight officers who may have been playing safe. The author's ancestor is mentioned in the fourth line, thus bringing a long search to a very satisfactory conclusion.

'Same old place                 Postmark
Friday night'                   'S.E.
                                   7.30pm
                                   25 Feb 16'

*Dear Mabel,*

*Just a line to let you know I am going home on pass from tonight until Monday at Noon. What do you think of the Workshop lads on the back. Writing later.*

*Howard*

Fig. 9. 'Same old place' is almost certainly Grove Park, S.E. London.

Fig. 10. (Reverse of Fig. 9.) Probably taken at the end of training. A class was usually eight trainees.

Fig. 11. The first postcard from France.

Fig. 12. Taken after the war.

Besides the medal with the regimental number, Figs. 9-12 show all that was available in hard evidence to trace the author's father.

Figure 13. No. 1955 Private William Ensor Dalgleish of the 1/6th Black Watch, June 1915.

Figure 14. A Quarter Master of the Army Service Corps.

Figure 15. An officer, lance corporal and two privates of the Royal Army Medical Corps in tropical uniform.

Figure 16. A private in the 7th Battalion of the Hampshire Regiment in marching order. He is wearing the distinctive cap badge of his battalion, one of the few Territorial Battalions to have their own cap badge.

# ABBREVIATIONS USED IN THE TEXT

It will soon be obvious to the researcher that abbreviations are not the invention of the second half of the 20th Century. A glance at Fig. 8 will prove the point. During the course of the research, most abbreviations will become familiar, especially those applying to the branch of the Army concerned. However, the reader may find the list below a helpful start as most appear in the text. For uniformity, all initials appear without the interposed full stop. During the war no one style was universally used.

| | |
|---|---|
| ADS | Advanced Dressing Station, a first aid post. |
| APS | Army Postal Service. |
| ASC | Army Service Corps. (Became RASC, Royal Army Service Corps, in 1919.) |
| AVS | Army Veterinary Service. |
| Bn.,Bns. | Battalion(s). A unit of approximately 1,000 infantry. |
| BEF | British Expeditionary Force, the term used to describe the British Army in France. |
| Ref. | Refers to the Bibliography (page 47). |
| CCS | Casualty Clearing Station. An 800-bed tented hospital run by a Royal Army Medical Corps unit. |
| CO | Commanding Officer. |
| Coy., Cos. | Company, companies. |
| DDMS | Deputy Director of Medical Services. |
| Div. | Division. A unit of approximately 18,000 men. |
| Divnl. | Divisional. Attached to, or concerned with, a Division. |
| FA | Field Ambulance. An RAMC unit; not a vehicle. |
| GHQ | General Headquarters. Used for both the location and organisation. |
| HQ | Headquarters. Used for both the location and organisation. |
| i/c | as in 'Officer i/c'. The Officer in Command of the unit in question. |
| IWM | Imperial War Museum, London. |
| L of C | Lines of Communication. |
| MAC | Motor Ambulance Convoy. An RAMC unit. |
| MGC | Machine Gun Corps. |
| NCO | Non-Commissioned Officer, e.g. Sergeant or Corporal. |
| RA | Royal Artillery. (Colloquially, The Gunners.) |
| RAMC | Royal Army Medical Corps. |
| RAOC | Royal Army Ordnance Corps. |
| RE | Royal Engineers. (Colloquially, The Sappers.) |
| RN | Royal Navy. |
| TNA | The National Archives (formerly the Public Record Office) |